# KS2 MATHS
## SATs SUCCESS
### PRACTICE TEST PAPERS

**Ages 10–11**

**KS2 MATHS SATs**

**2 complete tests**

**PRACTICE TEST PAPERS**

**TOM HALL**

# Contents

**Introduction and instructions** .................................................................... 3

**Set A**
Paper 1: arithmetic ........................................................................................ 5
Paper 2: reasoning ...................................................................................... 20
Paper 3: reasoning ...................................................................................... 33

**Set B**
Paper 1: arithmetic ...................................................................................... 46
Paper 2: reasoning ...................................................................................... 61
Paper 3: reasoning ...................................................................................... 74

**Answers and mark scheme** ..................................................................... 89
*(pull-out section at the back of the book)*

# Introduction and instructions

## How these tests will help your child

This book is made up of two complete sets of practice test papers. Each set contains similar test papers to those that your child will take in maths at the end of Year 6. They can be used any time throughout the year to provide practice for the Key Stage 2 tests.

The results of both sets of papers will provide a good idea of the strengths and weaknesses of your child.

## Administering the tests

- Provide your child with a quiet environment where they can complete each test undisturbed.
- Provide your child with a pen or pencil, ruler, eraser and protractor. A calculator is **not** allowed.
- The amount of time given for each paper varies, so remind your child at the start of each one how long they have and give them access to a clock or watch.
- You should only read the instructions out to your child, not the actual questions.
- Although handwriting is not assessed, remind your child that their answers should be clear.
- Advise your child that if they are unable to do one of the questions they should go on to the next one and come back to it later, if they have time. If they finish before the end, they should go back and check their work.

### Paper 1: arithmetic

- Answers are worth 1 or 2 marks, with a total number of 40 marks. Long multiplication and long division questions are worth 2 marks each. A mark may be awarded for showing the correct method.
- Your child will have **30 minutes** to answer the questions as quickly and carefully as they can.
- Encourage your child to look at the number of marks after each question to help them find out how much detail is required in their answer.
- Where questions are expressed as common fractions, the answers should be given as common fractions. All other answers should be given as whole or decimal numbers.

### Paper 2 and Paper 3: reasoning

- Answers are worth 1, 2 or 3 marks, with a total number of 35 marks. A mark may be awarded for showing the correct method in specific questions where there is a method box.
- Your child will have **40 minutes** to answer the questions as quickly and carefully as they can.
- Encourage your child to look at the number of marks after each question to help them find out how much detail is required in their answer.
- If your child needs to do some working out, advise them that they can use the space around the question.

## Marking the practice test papers

The answers and mark scheme have been provided to enable you to check how your child has performed. Fill in the marks that your child achieved for each part of the tests.

**Please note:** these tests are **only a guide** to the standard or mark your child can achieve and cannot guarantee the same is achieved during the Key Stage 2 tests, as the mark needed to achieve the expected standard varies from year to year.

|  | Set A | Set B |
| --- | --- | --- |
| Paper 1: arithmetic | /40 | /40 |
| Paper 2: reasoning | /35 | /35 |
| Paper 3: reasoning | /35 | /35 |
| Total | /110 | /110 |

The scores achieved on these practice test papers will help to show if your child is working at the expected standard in maths:
35–54 = working towards the expected standard
55–74 = working at the expected standard
75–110 = working above the expected standard.

When an area of weakness has been identified, it is useful to go over it and to look at similar types of questions with your child. Sometimes your child will be familiar with the subject matter but might not understand what the question is asking. This will become apparent when talking to your child.

## Shared marking and target setting

Engaging your child in the marking process will help them to develop a greater understanding of the tests and, more importantly, provide them with some ownership of their learning. They will be able to see more clearly how and why certain areas have been identified for them to target for improvement.

## Top tips for your child

**Don't make silly mistakes.** Make sure you emphasise to your child the importance of reading the question. Easy marks can be picked up by just doing as the question asks.

**Make answers clearly legible.** If your child has made a mistake, encourage them to put a cross through it and write the correct answer clearly next to it. Try to encourage your child to use an eraser as little as possible.

**Don't panic!** These practice test papers, and indeed the end of Key Stage 2 tests, are meant to provide a guide to the standard a child has attained. They are not the be-all and end-all, as children are assessed regularly throughout the school year. Explain to your child that there is no need to worry if they cannot do a question – tell them to go on to the next question and come back to the problematic question later if they have time.

# Key Stage 2

## Maths

### Paper 1: arithmetic

SET A

Maths

PAPER 1

You **may not** use a calculator to answer any questions in this test paper.

**Time:**

You have **30 minutes** to complete this test paper.

| Maximum mark | Actual mark |
|---|---|
| 40 | |

| First name | |
|---|---|
| Last name | |
| Date of birth | Day   Month   Year |

**1** 43 × 5 =

1 mark

**2** 574 + 56 =

1 mark

**3** 1,234 + 100 =

1 mark

**4** $\frac{2}{5} + \frac{2}{5} =$

1 mark

**5** ☐ = 9,999 − 1,000

1 mark

**6** 868 + 130 =

1 mark

**7** 607 × 3 =

1 mark

**8** 8.1 ÷ 10 =

1 mark

**9** 316 + 86 =

1 mark

**10** $5^2 =$

1 mark

**11** $492 \div 3 =$

1 mark

**12** ☐ $= \dfrac{9}{10} - \dfrac{1}{5}$

1 mark

**13** 10 − 15 =

1 mark

**14** $\frac{1}{2} + \frac{2}{5} =$

1 mark

**15** $\frac{1}{3} \times 24 =$

1 mark

**16** $\frac{1}{2} \div 4 =$

1 mark

**17** ☐ $= 0.6 \times 4$

1 mark

**18** 50% of 2,500 =

1 mark

**19** 50 − 5 × 10 =

**20** 5,725 + 3,750 =

**21** 5,804 − 5,075 =

**22** 47.32 − 15.44 =

1 mark

**23** 486.48 − 39.57 =

1 mark

**24** Show your method

```
    3 4
×   2 6
```

2 marks

**25** Show your method

```
2 3 ) 5 5 2
```

2 marks

14

**26** 30.75 × 100 =

1 mark

**27** $\frac{3}{4} + \frac{4}{12} =$

1 mark

**28** 78.7 − 65.88 =

1 mark

29  ☐ = 65 ÷ 100

30  50.806 − 32.661 =

**31** Show your method

```
    5 7 3
  ×   4 5
```

2 marks

**32** $\frac{3}{5} \div 4 =$

1 mark

**33**

Show your method

3 5 | 8 7 5

2 marks

**34**

$40 \times 1\frac{1}{2} =$

1 mark

35. $\frac{1}{3} \times \frac{1}{5} =$

36. 56.77 − 5.777 =

SET A

Maths

PAPER 2

# Key Stage 2

## Maths

### Paper 2: reasoning

You **may not** use a calculator to answer any questions in this test paper.

**Time:**

You have **40 minutes** to complete this test paper.

| Maximum mark | Actual mark |
|---|---|
| 35 | |

| First name | |
|---|---|
| Last name | |
| Date of birth | Day      Month      Year |

**1** This is part of a number square.

Circle all the numbers that have a remainder of 1 when divided by 4.

| 12 | 13 | 14 | 15 | 16 |
| --- | --- | --- | --- | --- |
| 22 | 23 | 24 | 25 | 26 |
| 32 | 33 | 34 | 35 | 36 |
| 42 | 43 | 44 | 45 | 46 |
| 52 | 53 | 54 | 55 | 56 |

2 marks

**2** Draw a pentagon with a pair of parallel lines.

Use a ruler.

2 marks

**3** Ellie and Rosie each buy one pizza.

Ellie eats $\frac{5}{8}$ of her pizza.

Rosie eats $\frac{7}{8}$ of her pizza.

What fraction of one pizza is left?

1 mark

**4** Tick (✔) the two numbers that have a difference of 1000.

32,658 ☐

33,758 ☐

33,768 ☐

34,758 ☐

43,858 ☐

1 mark

**5** Write the missing digits in this calculation.

```
      5 ☐ 4 ☐
   +  ☐ 5 ☐ 4
   ─────────────
      1 2 6 0 0
```

1 mark

**6** Calculate the perimeter of this shape.

☐ cm

1 mark

**7** A number squared and a number cubed both equal 64.

Find the numbers.

☐² = 64 = ☐³

1 mark

**8** Four hundred and sixty thousand, three hundred and five

Write this number in digits.

1 mark

**9** Reflect the shape in the mirror line.

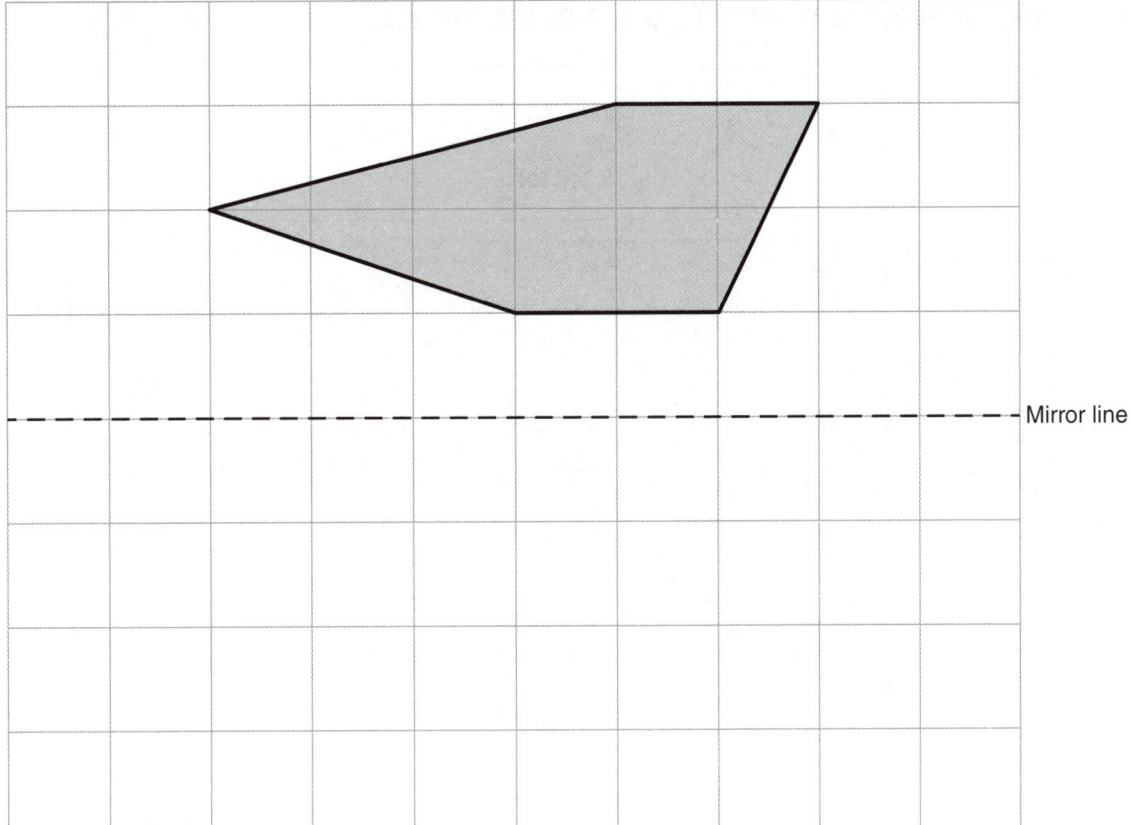

1 mark

**10** This table gives approximate conversions between kilograms and pounds.

| kilograms | pounds |
|---|---|
| 1 | 2.2 |
| 2 | 4.4 |
| 4 | 8.8 |
| 8 | 17.6 |
| 16 | 35.2 |

Use the table to convert 7 kilograms into pounds.

pounds

1 mark

Use the table to convert 22 pounds into kilograms.

kg

1 mark

**11** This is the plan of a football ground which has seats for 48,139 spectators.

The number of seats is shown for three of the stands.

How many seats are there in the South Stand?

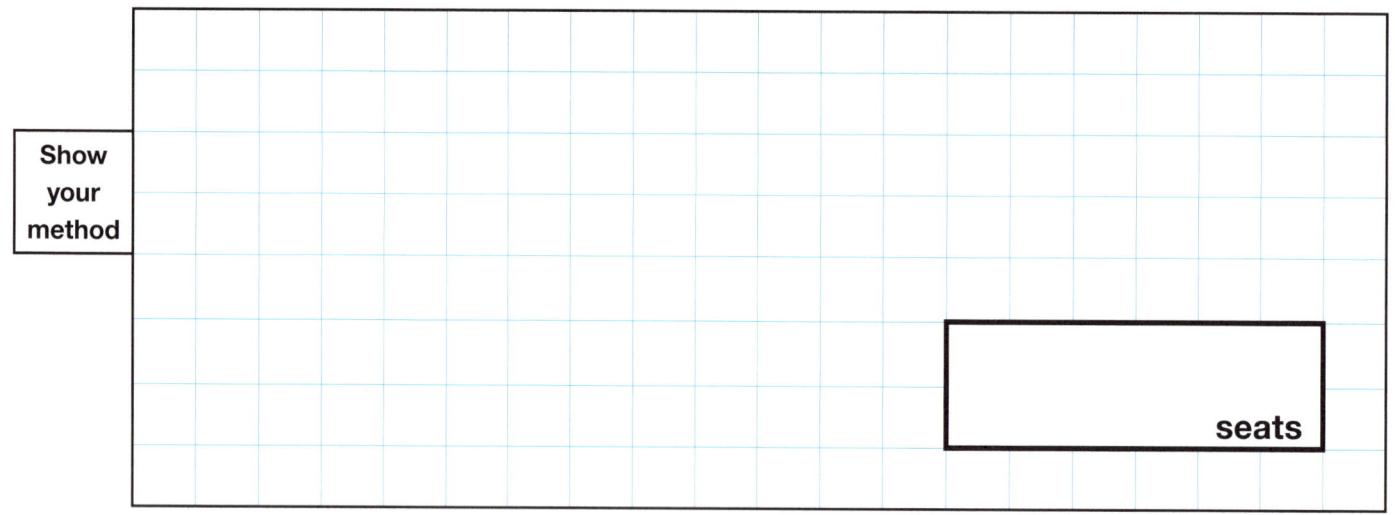

_____ seats

2 marks

**12** Tick (✔) the largest number.

56.276    56.093    56.239    56.198    56.273

☐         ☐         ☐         ☐         ☐

1 mark

**13** Tom has a collection of football cards.

Tom has 5 coloured cards to every 3 black and white cards.

He has 36 black and white cards.

Tom gives $\frac{1}{5}$ of his coloured cards to Jack.

How many cards does Tom give to Jack?

Show your method

cards

2 marks

**14** 330 ÷ 8 =

Give your answer as a decimal.

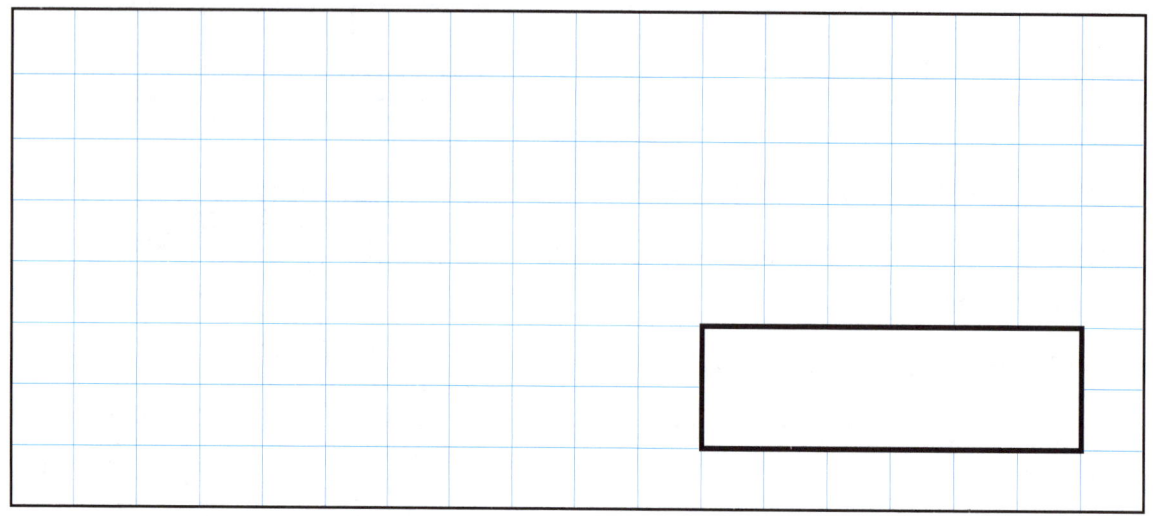

1 mark

**15** Oakview School has 460 pupils.

40% are girls.

Sea Lane School has 240 pupils.

60% are girls.

How many more girls are there at Oakview School?

Show your method

3 marks

**16** Find the value of 5a – 2b, when a = 5 and b = 7.

1 mark

Find the value of 5a + 2b, when a = 7 and b = 5.

1 mark

**17** Here are two equations with missing numbers.

☐ + △ = 18

☐ − △ = 6

Work out the value of the missing numbers.

☐ =

△ =

2 marks

**18** Here are four containers holding some water.

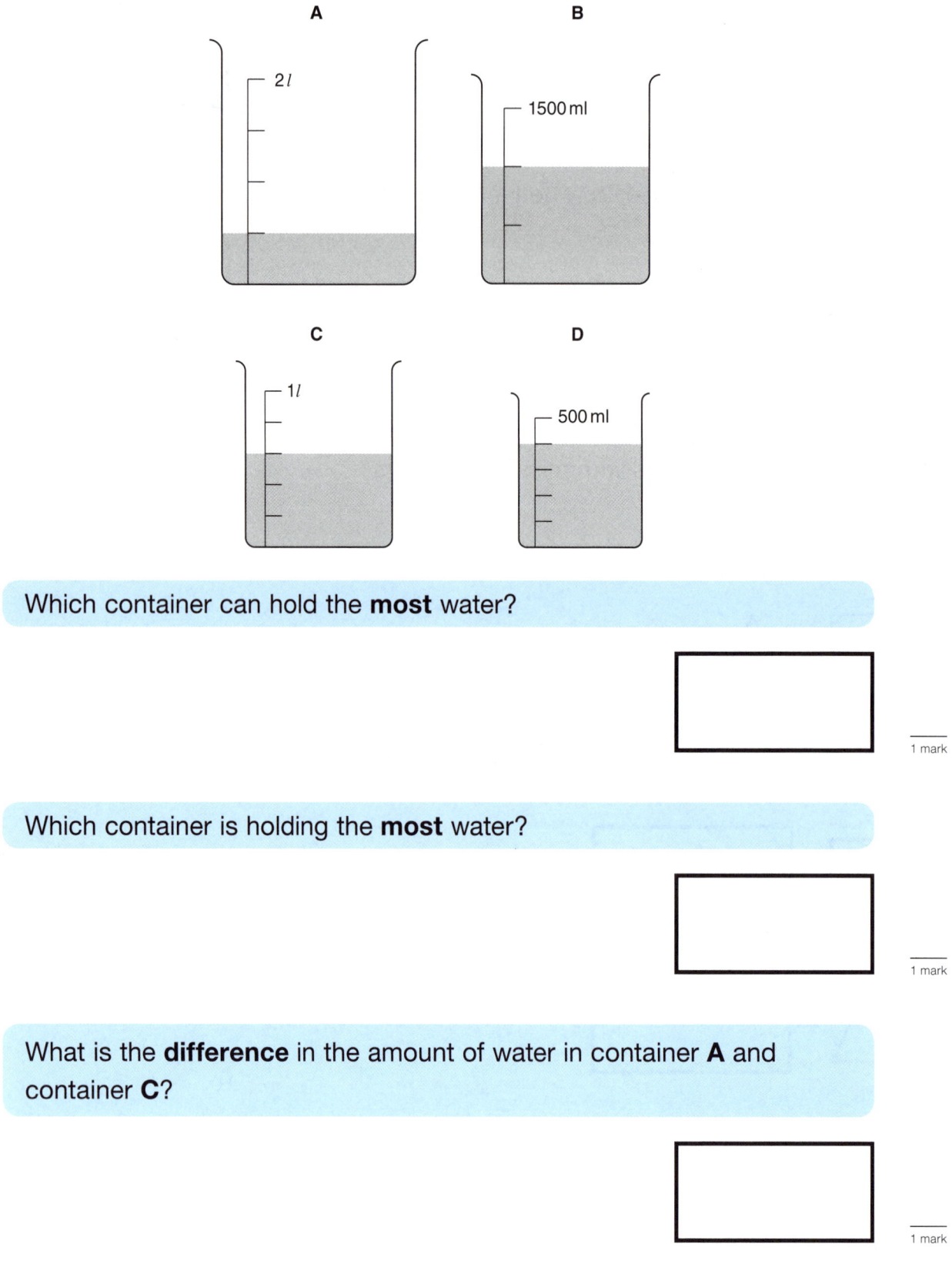

Which container can hold the **most** water?

1 mark

Which container is holding the **most** water?

1 mark

What is the **difference** in the amount of water in container **A** and container **C**?

1 mark

**19** Tick (✔) the circle with a radius drawn as a dashed line.

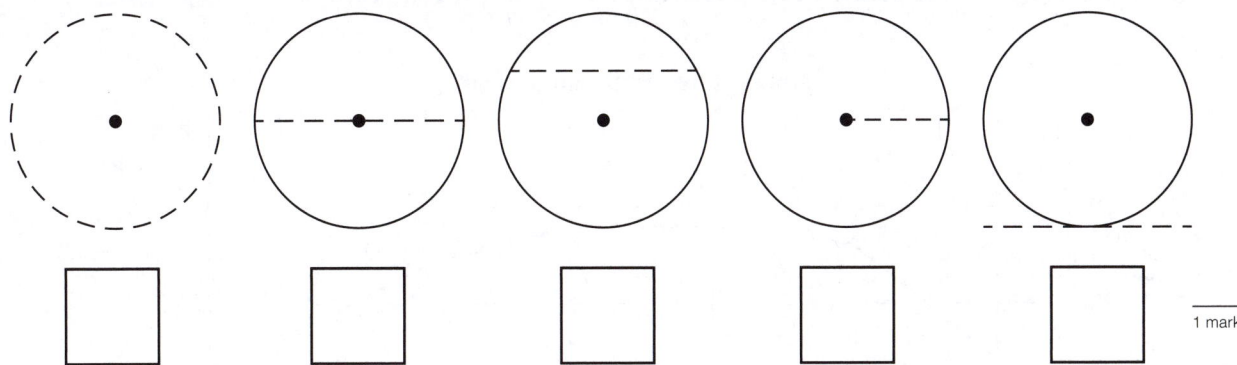

1 mark

**20** Here is a set of numbers.

7    15    24    30    48    53

Which two numbers are **common multiples** of 3 and 4?

1 mark

Which two numbers are **common factors** of 60?

1 mark

Which two numbers are **prime numbers**?

and

1 mark

**21** Sally wants to go on holiday to Spain.

She compares the mean temperatures for UK and Spain.

How much **warmer** was it in Spain than in UK in September?

1 mark

Sally wants to go to Spain when it is closest to 25°C.

Which **two** months could Sally choose?

_____

1 mark

# Key Stage 2

SET **A**

Maths

## Maths

### Paper 3: reasoning

PAPER 3

You **may not** use a calculator to answer any questions in this test paper.

**Time:**

You have **40 minutes** to complete this test paper.

| Maximum mark | Actual mark |
|---|---|
| 35 | |

| First name | |
|---|---|
| Last name | |
| Date of birth | Day | Month | Year |

© 2018 Letts Educational, an imprint of HarperCollinsPublishers Ltd – not to be photocopied.

33

**1** What number is shown by this abacus?

1 mark

**2** Find the missing number.

9 × ☐ = 72 ÷ 2

1 mark

**3** What time is shown on this clock?

1 mark

**4** Part of this shape is missing.

The dotted line is a line of symmetry.

Complete the shape.

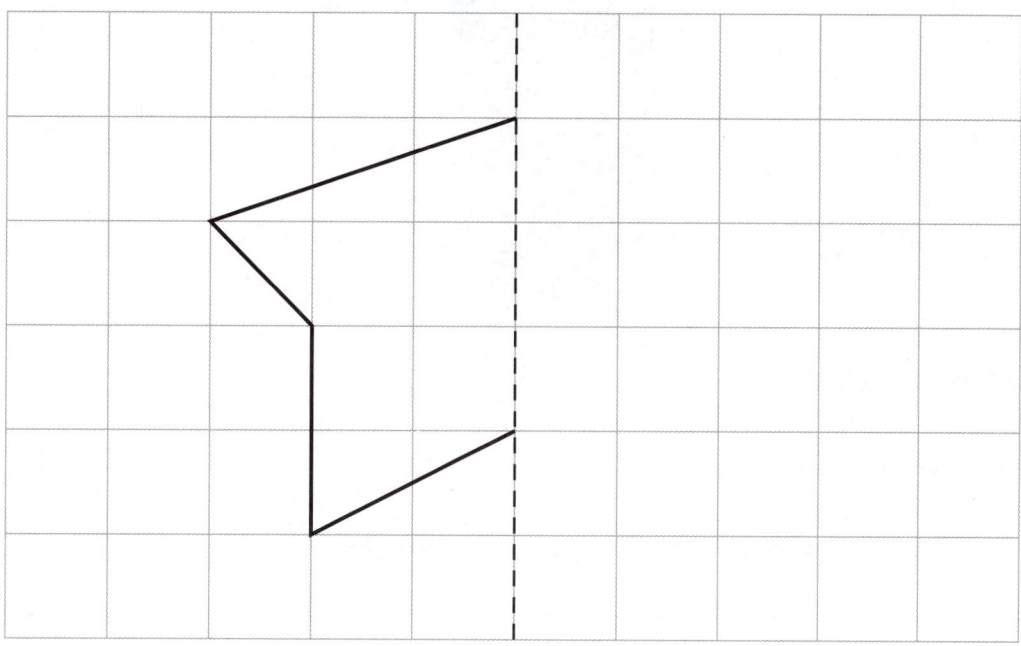

1 mark

Draw the line of symmetry on this shape.

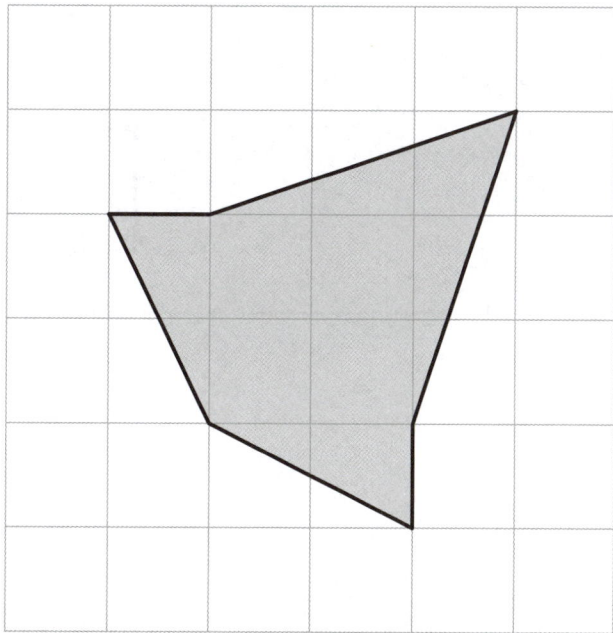

1 mark

**5** Chloe has 217 minutes left on her phone.

She uses 83 minutes.

She gets another 350 minutes.

How many minutes does Chloe have on her phone now?

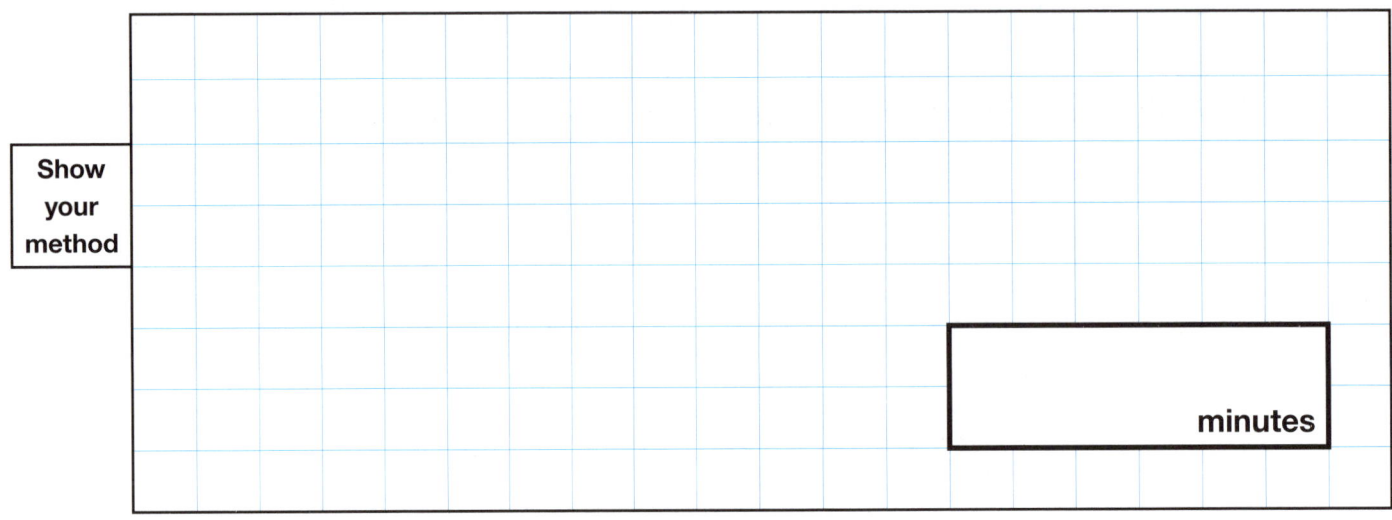

minutes

2 marks

**6** Tom buys 5 identical books for a total of £26.

What is the cost of each book?

£

1 mark

**7** 1 inch is about 2.5 centimetres.

How many centimetres is 12 inches?

cm

1 mark

There are 12 inches in 1 foot.

There are 3 feet in 1 yard.

Is 1 yard shorter or longer than 1 metre? Explain how you know.

1 mark

**8** The temperature outside a greenhouse is −4°C.

The temperature inside the greenhouse is 4°C.

What is the **difference** between the two temperatures?

☐ °C

1 mark

**9** Two prime numbers total 31.

What are the two numbers?

☐ ☐

1 mark

List the prime numbers that are greater than 40 and less than 50.

☐ ☐ ☐

1 mark

**10** Manisha has 24 counters.

- $\frac{1}{4}$ of the counters are red.
- $\frac{1}{3}$ of the counters are blue.
- $\frac{3}{8}$ of the counters are green.

The rest of the counters are yellow.

How many yellow counters are there?

Show your method

2 marks

**11** 878,421 − 319,875 =

Round each number in this calculation to the nearest hundred thousand to work out an estimated answer.

1 mark

**12** For each number, give the value of the digit 8.

7,376,548

8,065,913

5,682,790

7,368,514

2 marks

**13** An aeroplane is flying at a height of 8,000 m.

The outside temperature is −45°C.

Inside the aeroplane the temperature is 18°C.

What is the **difference** between the two temperatures?

°C

1 mark

**14** The population of a city is 275,386.

- 54,895 are aged 65 and over.
- 143,706 are aged 18 to 64.

How many are aged under 18?

Show your method

2 marks

**15** Draw a line from each fraction to the common factor used to simplify it.

$\frac{24}{30}$     3

$\frac{21}{30}$     4

$\frac{28}{32}$     5

$\frac{20}{25}$     6

2 marks

**16** These two triangles are the same shape but different sizes.

Work out the lengths of the sides x and y.

x = ☐ cm

1 mark

y = ☐ cm

1 mark

**17** Write these masses in order, **heaviest** first.

| 2.5 kg | 200 g | 2.05 kg | 2,550 g | 2.005 kg |
|--------|-------|---------|---------|----------|
| ☐ | ☐ | ☐ | ☐ | ☐ |

1 mark

**18** Tick (✔) each box if the fact about the drawn shape is true.

|  | has at least 1 pair of parallel sides | has at least 1 pair of perpendicular sides |
|---|---|---|
| Right-angled triangle | ☐ | ☐ |
| Rectangle | ☐ | ☐ |
| Parallelogram | ☐ | ☐ |

3 marks

**19** Teachers asked 120 children where they would like to go on a school visit.

This pie chart shows where they chose to go.

**School visit**

- Castle
- Museum
- Art gallery
- River study

Estimate how many children chose to visit the castle.

1 mark

40 children chose the river study.

What size angle at the centre of the pie chart is needed to show the river study?

1 mark

Half the children chose either the river study or the art gallery.

How many children chose to visit the art gallery?

1 mark

**20** Abi sat 6 tests.

Her mean score was 45.

How many marks did Abi score **altogether**?

1 mark

**21** A formula to find the perimeter, *P*, of a rectangle is

$$P = 2l + 2w, \text{ where } l = \text{length and } w = \text{width}$$

Work out the length of a rectangle that has a perimeter of 80 cm and a width of 10 cm.

Show your method

cm

2 marks

SET B

Maths

PAPER 1

# Key Stage 2

## Maths

### Paper 1: arithmetic

You **may not** use a calculator to answer any questions in this test paper.

**Time:**

You have **30 minutes** to complete this test paper.

| Maximum mark | Actual mark |
|---|---|
| 40 | |

| First name | |
|---|---|
| Last name | |
| Date of birth | Day    Month    Year |

**1** 40 ÷ 5 =

1 mark

**2** 828 − 102 =

1 mark

**3** $\frac{7}{8} - \frac{4}{8} =$

1 mark

**4** $\frac{1}{2} \times 30 =$

1 mark

**5** ☐ = 888 + 1,000

1 mark

**6** 855 + 477 =

1 mark

**7** 765 ÷ 5 =

1 mark

**8** 0.6 × 100 =

1 mark

**9** 2,705 + 7,808 =

1 mark

**10** ☐ = $3^3$

1 mark

**11** 4,088 × 6 =

1 mark

**12** 12.45 − 8.49 =

1 mark

**13** 0.03 × 6 =

1 mark

**14** $\frac{1}{2} - \frac{1}{10} =$

1 mark

**15** 4 − 12 =

1 mark

**16** ☐ = 325.8 + 4.67

1 mark

**17** 80,000 − 8,000 =

1 mark

**18** $\frac{1}{10} \div 2 =$

1 mark

**19** 9,360 − 745 =

1 mark

**20** 23.9 + 4.76 =

1 mark

**21** $5\frac{3}{4} - \frac{3}{8} =$

1 mark

**22** 20 × 30 × 40 =

1 mark

**23** 30% of 3,000 =

1 mark

**24** 75 ÷ 1,000 =

1 mark

**25** 654.23 − 40.8 =

1 mark

**26**

Show your method

```
    1 8 2
  ×   6 2
```

2 marks

**27** $100 \times 2\frac{1}{2} =$

1 mark

**28**

$22 \overline{)704}$

Show your method

2 marks

**29** 40 + 10 × 2 =

1 mark

**30**

7 1 ) 1 4 9 1

Show your method

2 marks

**31** $4\frac{2}{3} - 3\frac{3}{5} =$

1 mark

**32** 

$$\begin{array}{r} 3\,0\,7\,4 \\ \times \phantom{00}3\,5 \\ \hline \end{array}$$

Show your method

2 marks

**33** 4,000,000 − 400,000 =

1 mark

**34** 78.357 − 6.05 =

1 mark

**35** $\frac{3}{5}$ × 40 =

1 mark

**36** $\frac{2}{3} \div 2 =$

1 mark

# Key Stage 2

## Maths

### Paper 2: reasoning

**SET B**

Maths

PAPER 2

You **may not** use a calculator to answer any questions in this test paper.

**Time:**

You have **40 minutes** to complete this test paper.

| Maximum mark | Actual mark |
|---|---|
| 35 | |

| First name | |
|---|---|
| Last name | |
| Date of birth | Day　　　Month　　　Year |

© 2018 Letts Educational, an imprint of HarperCollinsPublishers Ltd – not to be photocopied.

**1** Tick (✔) the right angles in this shape.

1 mark

**2** Here are some counters.

What fraction of the counters are grey?

1 mark

**3** Dev read 26 books in a school year.

He drew a graph to show how many books he read each term.

Complete the bar for Term 3.

Dev's reading

(Bar chart: Term 1 = 7 books, Term 2 = 11 books, Term 3 = blank)

1 mark

**4** A train has 8 coaches.

Each coach has 72 seats.

The ticket collector says, 'I know 70 × 8 = 560'

What must he add to 560 to find how many seats there are in the train **altogether**?

1 mark

**5** Find the missing number.

$64 \times 24 = (64 \times 20) + (64 \times \boxed{\phantom{00}}) = 1{,}536$

1 mark

**6** A square is drawn on an empty grid.

The coordinates of three vertices are marked.

What are the coordinates of the fourth vertex?

(5, 10)
(5, 5)   (10, 5)

(___, ___)

1 mark

**7** A shop has a special offer.

Special offer!

Buy 3 tins of soup and get 1 free

Obi pays for 12 tins of soup.

How many tins does Obi get?

Show your method

2 marks

**8** Max makes some concrete for a path.

For a path 8 metres long Max needs:

- 200 kg of cement
- 600 kg of sand
- 600 kg of stone

What weight of stone will he need for a path 20 metres long?

Show your working

kg

2 marks

**9** Calculate the missing number.

56 × 9 = ☐ + 4

1 mark

Calculate the missing number.

56 + 64 = 3 × 4 × ☐

2 marks

**10** Here are some digit cards.

| 4 | 4 | 5 | 5 | 6 | 6 |

Use the digit cards to complete this equation.

Use each card only once.

☐☐☐ ÷ 100 = ☐.☐☐

1 mark

**11**

What is the **total** of angle A and angle B?

☐ °

1 mark

**12** Josh wants to buy tickets for a concert.

He needs 9 adult tickets and 3 child tickets.

> CONCERT
> Tickets
> Adult: £24.70
> Child: £18.50
>
> Group of 12: £249.99

How much will Josh save if he buys the group ticket?

Show your working

£ _____

3 marks

**13** Here are two fair triangular spinners.

Each spinner is spun once and the numbers added to give a total.

List the totals that can be made.

| | | | | |
|---|---|---|---|---|

2 marks

**14** This sequence decreases in equal steps.

Find the missing numbers.

6, −3, ☐, ☐, −30

2 marks

**15** Josef is thinking of a six-digit number.

Josef's number has:
- three hundred thousand
- seven hundred
- forty thousand
- All the other digits are 6.

Use these facts to complete the number.

| 3 | 4 | 6 | , | 7 | 6 | 6 |

1 mark

**16** This table shows the temperatures in five cities.

| City | London | Belfast | Manchester | Cardiff | Glasgow |
|---|---|---|---|---|---|
| Temperature | 4°C | 0°C | –3°C | –1°C | –5°C |

What is the **difference** between the temperatures in Manchester and Cardiff?

°C

1 mark

What is the **difference** between the warmest and coldest temperatures?

°C

1 mark

**17** Find the missing numerators in these equations.

$$\frac{3}{4} = \frac{\Box}{24}$$

$$\frac{5}{6} = \frac{\Box}{24}$$

$$\frac{3}{8} = \frac{\Box}{24}$$

$$\frac{2}{3} = \frac{\Box}{24}$$

2 marks

**18** What could the missing digits be?

$$\frac{1}{\Box} \times \frac{1}{\Box} = \frac{1}{16}$$

1 mark

$$\frac{\Box}{\Box} \times \frac{\Box}{\Box} = \frac{2}{8} = \frac{1}{4}$$

1 mark

**19** Dev and Sam share £45.

Dev takes half the amount Sam takes.

How much do they each take?

Dev takes £ [ ]

Sam takes £ [ ]

1 mark

**20** This rectangle has an area of 24 cm².

length [ ] cm and width [ ] cm

1 mark

length [ ] cm and width [ ] cm

1 mark

**21** Angles *x* and *y* are equal.

Calculate angle *x*.

*x* = ☐ °

1 mark

**22** Ben describes two shapes.

Name each shape.

> My first shape has four right angles and two pairs of sides of 10 cm and 5 cm.

_____

1 mark

> My second shape has four angles (two that are 120° and two that are 60°) and two pairs of sides that are 10 cm and 5 cm.

_____

1 mark

# Key Stage 2

**SET B**

Maths

PAPER 3

## Maths

### Paper 3: reasoning

You **may not** use a calculator to answer any questions in this test paper.

**Time:**

You have **40 minutes** to complete this test paper.

| Maximum mark | Actual mark |
|---|---|
| 35 | |

| First name | |
|---|---|
| Last name | |
| Date of birth | Day    Month    Year |

**1** Here are some digit cards:

| 3 | 4 | 5 | 6 | 7 |

Use the digits to make this correct.

Use each card once.

☐ ☐ ☐
+ ☐ ☐
―――――
6  0  1

2 marks

**2** This is a rectangle.

Tick (✔) **two** correct statements.

The two bold lines are perpendicular. ☐

The bold and thin lines are perpendicular. ☐

The two bold lines are parallel. ☐

The bold and thin lines are parallel. ☐

2 marks

**3** Dom sells computer games.

This pictogram shows the number of computer games he sold one week.

**Computer Game Sales**

⬤ stands for four computer games

| Sunday | ⬤ ⬤ ⬤ ⬤ |
| --- | --- |
| Monday | ⬤ ◖ |
| Tuesday | ⬤ ◔ |
| Wednesday | ⬤ |
| Thursday | ⬤ ⬤ ⬤ |
| Friday | ⬤ ⬤ ⬤ ◖ |
| Saturday | ⬤ ⬤ ⬤ ⬤ |

How many computer games did Dom sell in total on Friday and Saturday?

☐ games

1 mark

How many more games did Dom sell on Sunday than on Monday?

☐ games

1 mark

**4** Tick (✔) all the shapes that have $\frac{2}{3}$ shaded.

2 marks

76

**5** Ned has a 10 kg bag of potatoes.

He uses 2.3 kg of the potatoes one day.

He uses 1,600 g of the potatoes on the next day.

What is the weight of potatoes left?

Show your working

2 marks

**6** Translate the shape 7 squares right and 3 squares down.

2 marks

**7** Write the year MMXXII in digits.

1 mark

**8** Circle the number that is both:

- a factor of 36
- a multiple of 12

9      18      24      36      72

1 mark

**9** Round **196,704**

to the nearest ten

to the nearest thousand

to the nearest hundred thousand

2 marks

**10** Complete this table of equivalent fractions, decimals and percentages.

| Fraction | | Decimal | | Percentage |
|---|---|---|---|---|
| $\frac{65}{100}$ | = | | = | |
| | = | 0.8 | = | |
| | = | | = | 7% |

2 marks

**11** Write the following as digits.

one million, thirty-seven thousand, six hundred and four

1 mark

**12** Here are three digit cards.

| 1 | 2 | 3 |

Use each card to complete the missing digits in these sentences.

Use each card only once.

5 ☐   is a prime number.

4 ☐   is a common multiple of 3 and 7.

3 ☐   is a common factor of 62 and 93.

2 marks

**13** Find the missing digit.

$$\frac{2}{3} < \frac{\square}{12} < \frac{5}{6}$$

1 mark

**14** Tara thinks of a number, $n$.

She adds 12 to the number and then multiplies the answer by 3.

Tick (✔) the expression that shows this.

$3n + 12$ ☐

$3(n + 12)$ ☐

$3 \times 12 \times n$ ☐

$36 + n$ ☐

$n(3 + 12)$ ☐

1 mark

**15** Measure the marked angle using a protractor.

°

1 mark

**16** Sam sat two maths tests.

These were his scores:

Paper 1: $\frac{14}{20}$

Paper 2: $\frac{18}{25}$

Change Sam's fraction scores to percentage scores.

Paper 1: ☐ %

Paper 2: ☐ %

2 marks

**17** This pie chart shows the sports chosen by 80 children.

Here are some facts about the pie chart:

- 30 children chose tennis.
- $\frac{1}{4}$ of the children chose football.
- The same number of children chose gymnastics as chose rugby.

**School sports**

Football
Tennis
Rugby
Gymnastics

How many children chose rugby?

Show your working

children

2 marks

**18** Tick (✔) the number with 7 as the hundredths digit.

6.497 ☐

64.97 ☐ ✔

649.7 ☐

6,497 ☐

64,970 ☐

649,700 ☐

1 mark

**19** Work out the area of this triangle.

[Triangle with height 20 cm and base 15 cm]

[Answer box] cm²

1 mark

Work out the length of this parallelogram.

[Parallelogram with height 10 cm, Area = 400 cm²]

[Answer box] cm

1 mark

**20** The dots, A to F, can be joined to make a straight line.

The dots are drawn at regular intervals.

(8, 7) A
(4, 5) B
(0, 3) C
D
E
(−12, −3) F

Some dots have coordinates.

What are the coordinates of dots D and E?

D = (___, ___)

E = (___, ___)

2 marks

**21** Tickets to an amusement park cost £17.50 each.

There is a special offer. Eight tickets can be bought for £110.

How much cheaper is **each** ticket with the special offer?

Show your method

£

2 marks

# Answers

**Set A Paper 1**

1. 215 (1 mark)
2. 630 (1 mark)
3. 1,334 (1 mark)
4. $\frac{4}{5}$ (Accept equivalent fractions) (1 mark)
5. 8,999 (1 mark)
6. 998 (1 mark)
7. 1,821 (1 mark)
8. 0.81 (1 mark)
9. 402 (1 mark)
10. 25 (1 mark)
11. 164 (1 mark)
12. $\frac{7}{10}$ (Accept equivalent fractions) (1 mark)
13. −5 (Do not accept 5−) (1 mark)
14. $\frac{9}{10}$ (Accept equivalent fractions) (1 mark)
15. 8 (1 mark)
16. $\frac{1}{8}$ (Accept equivalent fractions) (1 mark)
17. 2.4 (1 mark)
18. 1,250 (1 mark)
19. 0 (1 mark)
20. 9,475 (1 mark)
21. 729 (1 mark)
22. 31.88 (1 mark)
23. 446.91 (1 mark)
24.
```
        3 4
    ×   2 6
      2 0 4
      6 8 0
      8 8 4
```
(2 marks for correct answer. Award 1 mark for using long multiplication with no more than one error but wrong answer given. Do not award any marks if the 0 for multiplying by a ten is missing. Do not award any marks if no final answer is given.)

25.
```
          2 4
    2 3 ) 5 5 2
          4 6
            9 2
            9 2
              0
```
(2 marks for correct answer. Award 1 mark for using long division with no more than one error but wrong answer given. Do not award any marks if no final answer is given.)

26. 3,075 (1 mark)
27. $1\frac{1}{12}$ (Accept equivalent fractions) (1 mark)
28. 12.82 (1 mark)
29. 0.65 (1 mark)
30. 18.145 (1 mark)

31.

|   |   | 5 | 7 | 3 |
|---|---|---|---|---|
|   | × |   | 4 | 5 |
|   | 2 | 8 | 6 | 5 |
| 2 | 2 | 9 | 2 | 0 |
| 2 | 5 | 7 | 8 | 5 |

(2 marks for correct answer. Award 1 mark for using long multiplication with no more than one error but wrong answer given. Do not award any marks if the 0 for multiplying by a ten is missing. Do not award any marks if no final answer is given.)

32. $\frac{3}{20}$ (Accept equivalent fractions) (1 mark)

33.

|   |   |   | 2 | 5 |
|---|---|---|---|---|
| 3 | 5 | 8 | 7 | 5 |
|   |   | 7 | 0 |   |
|   |   | 1 | 7 | 5 |
|   |   | 1 | 7 | 5 |
|   |   |   |   | 0 |

(2 marks for correct answer. Award 1 mark for using long division with no more than one error but wrong answer given. Do not award any marks if no final answer is given.)

34. 60 (1 mark)
35. $\frac{1}{15}$ (1 mark)
36. 50.993 (1 mark)

## Set A Paper 2

1. 13, 25, 33, 45 and 53 circled only.
(2 marks: 1 mark for three answers circled)

2. (2 marks: 1 mark for a shape with five sides; 1 mark for a pair of parallel lines)

3. $\frac{1}{2}$ (Accept $\frac{4}{8}$ or other equivalent fractions) (1 mark)

4. 33,758 and 34,758 ticked only.
(1 mark: 1 mark for both correct answers)

5.

|   | 5 | 0 | 4 | 6 |
|---|---|---|---|---|
| + | 7 | 5 | 5 | 4 |
| 1 | 2 | 6 | 0 | 0 |

(1 mark: all correct for 1 mark)

6. 64 cm (1 mark)
7. 8, 4 (1 mark)
8. 460,305 (1 mark)
9. (Accept lines drawn to within 2 mm of vertices) (1 mark)
10. 15.4 pounds (1 mark)
    10 kg (1 mark)
11. 12,316
(2 marks for correct answer. Award 1 mark for correct working with wrong answer.)
12. 56.276 ticked only. (1 mark)
13. 12
(2 marks for correct answer. Award 1 mark for correct working with wrong answer.)
14. 41.25 (1 mark)
15. 40
(3 marks for correct answer. Award 1 mark for finding 40% of 460 = 184 or 1 mark for finding 60% of 240 = 144 or 1 mark for a correct subtraction of the answers even if the percentages are incorrect.)

16. 11 **(1 mark)**
    45 **(1 mark)**
17. ☐ = 12, △ = 6
    **(2 marks for correct answer. Award 1 mark for ☐ = 6, △ = 12)**
18. A **(1 mark)**
    B **(1 mark)**
    100 ml or 0.1 *l* **(1 mark)**
19. 4th shape ticked only. **(1 mark)**
20. 24 and 48 **(1 mark)**
    15 and 30 **(1 mark)**
    7 and 53 **(1 mark)**
21. 13°C (Accept +/− 1°C) **(1 mark)**
    September and October **(1 mark)**

## Set A Paper 3

1. 640 **(1 mark)**
2. 4 **(1 mark)**
3. 7:20 (Accept 7:20 am, 7:20 pm, 19:20, 20 past 7) **(1 mark)**
4. (Accept lines drawn to within 2 mm of vertices. Ignore lines that are not straight.) **(1 mark)**

   (Accept lines drawn within 2 mm of the vertices.) **(1 mark)**
5. 217 − 83 = 134;
   134 + 350 = 484 minutes
   **(2 marks for correct answer. Award 1 mark for correct working, but wrong answer given.)**
6. £5.20 (Do not accept 5.2) **(1 mark)**
7. 30 cm **(1 mark)**
   Explanation should show that there are approximately 90 cm (3 × 30 cm) in 1 yard and 90 cm < 100 cm **(1 mark)**
8. 8°C **(1 mark)**
9. 2 and 29 (Accept answers in either order) **(1 mark)**
   41  43  47 **(1 mark)**
10. $(\frac{1}{4} \times 24) + (\frac{1}{3} \times 24) + (\frac{3}{8} \times 24) = 23$;
    6 + 8 + 9 = 23; 24 − 23 = 1
    **(2 marks for correct answer. Award 1 mark for correct working, but wrong answer given.)**
11. 600,000 (Do not accept 558,546) **(1 mark)**
12. 8 or eight units or eight ones
    8,000,000 or eight million
    80,000 or eighty thousand or eight ten thousands
    8,000 or eight thousand
    **(2 marks: 2 marks for four correct answers, 1 mark for two or three correct answers)**
13. 63°C **(1 mark)**
14. 275,386 − (54,895 + 143,706) = 76,785
    **(2 marks for correct answer. Award 1 mark for correct working, but wrong answer given.)**
15. $\frac{24}{30}$ — 3
    $\frac{21}{30}$ — 4
    $\frac{28}{32}$ — 5
    $\frac{20}{25}$ — 6
    **(2 marks: 2 marks for four lines correctly drawn, 1 mark for two or three lines correctly drawn)**

16. $x = 7.5$ cm **(1 mark)**
    $y = 15$ cm **(1 mark)**
17. 2,550 g   2.5 kg   2.05 kg
    2.005 kg   200 g (Accept units that have been converted correctly, e.g. 2,550 g   2,500 g   2,050 g   2005 g   200 g) **(1 mark)**
18. Right-angled triangle ☐ ✓
    Rectangle ✓ ✓
    Parallelogram ✓ ☐
    **(3 marks: 1 mark for each shape)**
19. 30 (Accept +/− 1) **(1 mark)**
    120° **(1 mark)**
    20 **(1 mark)**
20. 270 **(1 mark)**
21. $80 = 2l + 2 \times 10$; $80 = 2l + 20$;
    $60 = 2l$; $60 \div 2 = l = 30$ cm
    **(2 marks for correct answer. Award 1 mark for correct working, but wrong answer given.)**

## Set B Paper 1

1. 8 **(1 mark)**
2. 726 **(1 mark)**
3. $\frac{3}{8}$ (Accept equivalent fractions) **(1 mark)**
4. 15 **(1 mark)**
5. 1,888 **(1 mark)**
6. 1,332 **(1 mark)**
7. 153 **(1 mark)**
8. 60 **(1 mark)**
9. 10,513 **(1 mark)**
10. 27 **(1 mark)**
11. 24,528 **(1 mark)**
12. 3.96 **(1 mark)**
13. 0.18 **(1 mark)**
14. $\frac{2}{5}$ (Accept $\frac{4}{10}$ and other equivalent fractions) **(1 mark)**
15. −8 (Do not accept 8−) **(1 mark)**
16. 330.47 **(1 mark)**
17. 72,000 **(1 mark)**
18. $\frac{1}{20}$ (Accept equivalent fractions) **(1 mark)**
19. 8,615 **(1 mark)**
20. 28.66 **(1 mark)**
21. $5\frac{3}{8}$ (Accept equivalent fractions. Accept $\frac{43}{8}$) **(1 mark)**
22. 24,000 **(1 mark)**
23. 900 **(1 mark)**
24. 0.075 **(1 mark)**
25. 613.43 **(1 mark)**
26. 

|   |   | 1 | 8 | 2 |
|---|---|---|---|---|
|   | × |   | 6 | 2 |
|   |   | 3 | 6 | 4 |
| 1 | 0 | 9 | 2 | 0 |
| 1 | 1 | 2 | 8 | 4 |

**(2 marks for correct answer. Award 1 mark for using long multiplication with no more than one error but wrong answer given. Do not award any marks if the 0 for multiplying by a ten is missing. Do not award any marks if no final answer is given.)**

27. 250 **(1 mark)**
28. 

|   |   |   | 3 | 2 |
|---|---|---|---|---|
| 2 | 2 | 7 | 0 | 4 |
|   |   | 6 | 6 |   |
|   |   |   | 4 | 4 |
|   |   |   | 4 | 4 |
|   |   |   |   | 0 |

**(2 marks for correct answer. Award 1 mark for using long division with no more than one error but wrong answer given. Do not award any marks if no final answer is given.)**

29. 60 **(1 mark)**

30.

```
          2 1
    ┌─────────
7 1 │ 1 4 9 1
      1 4 2
      ─────
          7 1
          7 1
          ───
            0
```

(2 marks for correct answer. Award 1 mark for using long division with no more than one error but wrong answer given. Do not award any marks if no final answer is given.)

31. $1\frac{1}{15}$ (Accept equivalent fractions) (1 mark)

32.

```
      3 0 7 4
    ×     3 5
    ─────────
    1 5 3 7 0
    9 2 2 2 0
    ─────────
  1 0 7 5 9 0
```

(2 marks for correct answer. Award 1 mark for using long multiplication with no more than one error but wrong answer given. Do not award any marks if the 0 for multiplying by a ten is missing. Do not award any marks if no final answer is given.)

33. 3,600,000 (1 mark)
34. 72.307 (1 mark)
35. 24 (1 mark)
36. $\frac{1}{3}$ (Accept equivalent fractions) (1 mark)

**Set B Paper 2**

1. (1 mark: all three right angles needed for 1 mark)

2. $\frac{3}{5}$ (Accept equivalent fractions, e.g. $\frac{6}{10}$. Accept 0.6 or 60%) (1 mark)

3. A bar or line drawn to show 8 (1 mark)

4. 16 or 2 × 8 (1 mark)
5. 4 (1 mark)
6. (10, 10) (1 mark)
7. 12 ÷ 3 = 4; 12 + 4 = 16 tins

(2 marks for correct answer. Award 1 mark for correct working, but wrong answer given.)

8. 20 ÷ 8 = 2.5; 600 × 2.5 = 1500 kg

(2 marks for correct answer. Award 1 mark for correct working, but wrong answer given.)

9. 500 (1 mark)
10

(2 marks for correct answer. Award 1 mark for sight of: 56 + 64 = 120 or 3 × 4 = 12 or 120 ÷ 12)

10. Accept any correct answer, e.g.
456 ÷ 100 = 4.56; 465 ÷ 100 = 4.65;
546 ÷ 100 = 5.46; 564 ÷ 100 = 5.64;
645 ÷ 100 = 6.45; 654 ÷ 100 = 6.54
(1 mark)

11. 180° (1 mark)
12. £27.81

(3 marks for correct answer. Award 1 mark for a correct method of finding the cost of 9 adult and 3 child tickets with a wrong answer and award 1 mark for a correct method of finding the difference between the cost of the individual tickets and the group ticket with a wrong answer.)

13. 5  6  7  8  9

(2 marks: 2 marks for five correct answers, 1 mark for three or four correct answers)

14. −12   −21

(2 marks: 1 mark for each correct answer)

15. 346,766 (1 mark)

16. 2°C (1 mark)
    9°C (1 mark)
17. $\frac{3}{4} = \frac{18}{24}$

    $\frac{3}{8} = \frac{9}{24}$

    $\frac{5}{6} = \frac{20}{24}$

    $\frac{2}{3} = \frac{16}{24}$

    **(2 marks: 2 marks for four correct answers, 1 mark for two or three correct answers)**
18. Accept $\frac{1}{2} \times \frac{1}{8}$ or $\frac{1}{8} \times \frac{1}{2}$ or $\frac{1}{4} \times \frac{1}{4}$ or $\frac{1}{1} \times \frac{1}{16}$ (1 mark)

    $\frac{1}{2} \times \frac{2}{4}$ or $\frac{1}{1} \times \frac{2}{8}$ (Accept for either calculation numerators or denominators reversed) (1 mark)
19. Dev takes £15
    Sam takes £30 (1 mark)
20. Possible answers are:
    length  24 cm     width  1 cm
    length  12 cm     width  2 cm
    length  6 cm      width  4 cm
    (Accept lengths and widths reversed. Accept fractions and decimals if correct, e.g. 48 cm × 0.5 cm. Do not accept length 3 cm, width 8 cm)
    **(2 marks: 1 mark for each pair of correct answers)**
21. 135° (1 mark)
22. rectangle (Accept oblong) (1 mark)
    parallelogram (1 mark)

**Set B Paper 3**
1. Possible answers: 567 + 34, 564 + 37, 537 + 64, 534 + 67
   **(2 marks: 1 mark for correct placing of 7 and 4 in the units column)**
2. 2nd and 3rd boxes ticked only.
   **(2 marks: 1 mark for each correct box ticked)**
3. 29 games (1 mark)
   10 games (1 mark)
4. 1st and 4th shapes ticked only.
   **(2 marks: 1 mark for each correct box ticked)**
5. 10 − (2.3 + 1.6) = 6.1 kg or 10,000 − (2,300 + 1,600) = 6,100 g (Accept 6.1 kg or 6100 g. Units must be correct, e.g. do not accept 6.1 g or 6,100 kg. Accept 6,100 or 6.1 without units.)
   **(2 marks for correct answer. Award 1 mark for correct working, but wrong answer given.)**
6. 

   **(2 marks: 2 marks for drawing as shown; 1 mark for correctly orientated and sized shape translated 7 units right or 3 units down)**
7. 2022 (1 mark)
8. 36 circled only. (1 mark)
9. 196,700
   197,000
   200,000
   **(2 marks: 2 marks for three correct, 1 mark for two correct)**

10.

| Fraction | | Decimal | | Percentage |
|---|---|---|---|---|
| $\frac{65}{100}$ | = | 0.65 | = | 65% |
| $\frac{4}{5}$ or equivalent | = | 0.8 | = | 80% |
| $\frac{7}{100}$ | = | 0.07 | = | 7% |

**(2 marks: 2 marks for six correct answers, 1 mark for four or five correct answers)**

11. 1,037,604 (Accept misplaced commas) **(1 mark)**
12. 53
    42
    31
    **(2 marks: 2 marks for three correct answers, 1 mark for two correct answers)**
13. 9 **(1 mark)**
14. 2nd box ticked only. **(1 mark)**
15. 55° (Accept angles within 2°) **(1 mark)**
16. Paper 1    70%
    Paper 2    72% **(2 marks)**
17. $\dfrac{80 - (\frac{1}{4} \times 80 + 30)}{2}$ = 15 children

    **(2 marks for correct answer. Award 1 mark for correct working, but wrong answer given.)**
18. 2nd box ticked only. **(1 mark)**
19. 150 cm² **(1 mark)**
    40 cm **(1 mark)**
20. D    (−4, 1)
    E    (−8, −1)
    **(2 marks: 1 mark for each coordinate)**
21. £17.50 − (£110 ÷ 8) = £17.50 − £13.75 = £3.75

    **(2 marks for correct answer. Award 1 mark for correct working, but wrong answer given.)**

# Letts
## gets you through

# KS2 ENGLISH
## SATs SUCCESS
## PRACTICE TEST PAPERS

Ages 10–11

**KS2 ENGLISH SATs**

4 complete tests

**PRACTICE TEST PAPERS**

## SHELLEY WELSH AND LAURA GRIFFITHS

# Contents

**Introduction and instructions** ................................................................. 3

**Set A**
English reading paper answer booklet ..................................................... 5
English grammar, punctuation and spelling Paper 1: questions ............ 20
English grammar, punctuation and spelling Paper 2: spelling ................ 34

**Set B**
English reading paper answer booklet ..................................................... 37
English grammar, punctuation and spelling Paper 1: questions ............ 52
English grammar, punctuation and spelling Paper 2: spelling ................ 66

**English reading booklets** ...................................................................... 73
**Answers and mark scheme** .................................................................. 93
**Spelling test administration** ................................................................. 101

*(pull-out section at the back of the book)*

# Introduction and instructions

## How these tests will help your child

This book is made up of two sets of practice test papers. Each set contains similar test papers to those that your child will take at the end of Year 6 in English reading and English grammar, punctuation and spelling. They can be used any time throughout the year to provide practice for the Key Stage 2 tests.

The results of both sets of papers will provide a good idea of the strengths and weaknesses of your child.

## Administering the tests

- Provide your child with a quiet environment where they can complete each test undisturbed.
- Provide your child with a pen or pencil, ruler and eraser.
- The amount of time given for each test varies, so remind your child at the start of each one how long they have and give them access to a clock or watch.
- You should only read the instructions out to your child, not the actual questions (except where instructed otherwise).
- Although handwriting is not assessed, remind your child that their answers should be clear.

## English reading

- Each test is made up of three different texts and an answer booklet.
- Answers are worth 1, 2 or 3 marks, with a total number of 50 marks for each test.
- Your child will have **one hour** to read the texts in the reading booklet and answer questions in the answer booklet.
- Some questions are multiple choice, some are short answers where only a word or phrase is required, and others are longer and followed by several lines on which to write the answer.
- Encourage your child to look at the mark scheme after each question to help them know how much detail is required in their answer.

## English grammar, punctuation and spelling

### Paper 1: questions

- Each answer is worth 1 mark, with a total of 50 marks available.
- Your child will have **45 minutes** to complete the test paper.
- Some questions are multiple choice and may require a tick in the box next to the answer. Some require a word or phrase to be underlined or circled, while others have a line or box for the answer. Some questions ask for missing punctuation marks to be inserted.

### Paper 2: spelling

- Contains 20 spellings, with each spelling worth 1 mark.
- Your child will have approximately **15 minutes** to complete the test paper.
- Using the spelling test administration guide on pages 101–102, read each spelling and allow your child time to fill it in on their spelling paper.

## Marking the practice test papers

The answers and mark scheme have been provided to enable you to check how your child has performed. Fill in the marks that your child achieved for each part of the tests.

**Please note:** these tests are **only a guide** to the standard or mark your child can achieve and cannot guarantee the same is achieved during the Key Stage 2 tests, as the mark needed to achieve the expected standard varies from year to year.

## English reading

|  | Set A | Set B |
| --- | --- | --- |
| English reading paper | /50 | /50 |

The scores achieved on these practice test papers will help to show if your child is working at the expected standard in English reading: 13–25 = working towards the expected standard; 26–36 = working at the expected standard; 37–50 = working above the expected standard.

## English grammar, punctuation and spelling

|  | Set A | Set B |
| --- | --- | --- |
| Paper 1: questions | /50 | /50 |
| Paper 2: spelling | /20 | /20 |
| Total | /70 | /70 |

The scores achieved on these practice test papers will help to show if your child is working at the expected standard in English grammar, punctuation and spelling: 20–35 = working towards the expected standard; 36–50 = working at the expected standard; 51–70 = working above the expected standard.

When an area of weakness has been identified, it is useful to go over these, and similar types of questions, with your child. Sometimes your child will be familiar with the subject matter but might not understand what the question is asking. This will become apparent when talking to your child.

## Shared marking and target setting

Engaging your child in the marking process will help them to develop a greater understanding of the tests and, more importantly, provide them with some ownership of their learning. They will be able to see more clearly how and why certain areas have been identified for them to target for improvement.

## Top tips for your child

**Don't make silly mistakes.** Make sure you emphasise to your child the importance of reading the question. Easy marks can be picked up by just doing as the question asks.

**Make answers clearly legible.** If your child has made a mistake, encourage them to put a cross through it and write the correct answer clearly next to it. Try to encourage your child to use an eraser as little as possible.

**Don't panic!** These practice test papers, and indeed the Key Stage 2 tests, are meant to provide a guide to the standard a child has attained. They are not the be-all and end-all, as children are assessed regularly throughout the school year. Explain to your child that there is no need to worry if they cannot do a question – tell them to go on to the next question and come back to the problematic question later if they have time.

SET A

# Key Stage 2

## English reading

### Reading answer booklet

English reading

**Time:**

You have **one hour** to read the texts in the reading booklet (pages 75–83) and answer the questions in this answer booklet.

| Maximum mark | Actual mark |
|---|---|
| 50 | |

| First name | |
|---|---|
| Last name | |
| Date of birth | Day | Month | Year |

© 2018 Letts Educational, an imprint of HarperCollinsPublishers Ltd – not to be photocopied.

**Questions 1–17 are about *A Mad Tea Party* (see pages 76–77 in the reading booklet).**

**1** Where is the scene set?

_____

1 mark

**2** Why is Alice very small?

_____

1 mark

**3** Look at the opening conversation.

**Find** and **copy** the clause Alice says just before she sits down at the table.

_____

1 mark

**4** Which character offers Alice a drink?

Tick **one**.

| | |
|---|---|
| the Hare | ☐ |
| the Hatter | ☐ |
| the Narrator | ☐ |
| the Dormouse | ☐ |

1 mark

**5** Why is Alice angry?

_____

_____
1 mark

**6** **Alice:** *Then it wasn't very **civil** of you to offer it!*

What does the word *civil* mean in this line?

Tick **one**.

polite ☐

angry ☐

old ☐

rude ☐
1 mark

**7** Look at the Narrator's opening lines.

**Find** and **copy** the words that suggest Alice is correct in saying there is room for her to sit down.

_____

_____
1 mark

**8** Explain why Alice says, *'it's very rude!'*.

_____

_____
1 mark

**9** What stops the characters arguing?

_____

_____
1 mark

**10** Towards the end of the passage the Narrator says, *'The conversation drops'*.

What does the word *drops* mean in this context?

_____
1 mark

**11** Which adjective best describes Alice during the tea party?

Tick **one**.

| | |
|---|---|
| unconfident | ☐ |
| impressed | ☐ |
| amused | ☐ |
| frustrated | ☐ |

1 mark

**12** The Narrator refers to the Hatter as 'the Mad Hatter'.

What does the Hatter do that might make him appear 'mad'?

_____

_____

1 mark

**13** Look at the title of the extract: *A Mad Tea Party*.

Explain fully why this is an appropriate title, referring to the text in your answer.

_____

_____

_____

1 mark

**14** *The characters continue arguing until the Hatter opens his eyes very wide and begins talking in* **riddles***.*

Which word below is closest in meaning to *riddle*?

Tick **one**.

solution ☐

puzzle ☐

sentence ☐

argument ☐

1 mark

**15** Explain the role of the Narrator in the extract.

_____

_____
1 mark

**16** Write **one** word that refers to the mechanism of the Hatter's watch.

_____
1 mark

**17** **Hare:** (meekly) It was the *best* butter?

Why is the Hare's response to the Hatter funny?

_____
1 mark

**Questions 18–30 are about the *Isles of Scilly* (see pages 78–80 in the reading booklet).**

**18** What is the name of the largest island of the Isles of Scilly?

_____

1 mark

**19** *The Isles of Scilly are made up of five **inhabited** and approximately 140 other islands.*

What does the word *inhabited* mean?

Tick **one**.

deserted ☐

far away ☐

people live there ☐

tropical ☐

1 mark

**20** Look at the paragraph beginning: *To reach the Isles of Scilly from the mainland . . .*

Give **two** ways visitors can reach the islands.

1. _____

2. _____

1 mark

**21** Read the advantages and disadvantages of the two methods of transport. Which would you recommend for the following visitors?
Give reasons for your answers **using the information in the text**.

**A day visitor with no luggage:** _____

_____

_____

_____
1 mark

**A family who are staying for a week who want to see dolphins swimming:**

_____

_____

_____
1 mark

**22** Why are the Scilly Isles sometimes described as 'a large, natural greenhouse'?

_____

_____
1 mark

**23** Why might the Skybus flight be cancelled?

_____

_____
1 mark

**24** Compare how someone participating in and someone watching a gig race would be involved.

**Participating:** _____

_____
1 mark

**Watching:** _____

_____
1 mark

**25** List **three** activities that the leaflet suggests for tourists to do when visiting the Isles of Scilly.

1. _____

2. _____

3. _____
1 mark

**26** How do the locals usually travel around the islands? Give **two** ways of travelling around the islands.

1. _____

2. _____
1 mark

**27** In what format are you most likely to see this text?

Tick **one**.

a poster ☐

a travel leaflet ☐

a storybook ☐

a school magazine ☐

1 mark

**28** What is the effect of the words underlined in this sentence?

*The Isles of Scilly have many historic landmarks <u>waiting to be explored.</u>*

_____

_____

1 mark

**29** Put a tick in each row to show whether the statements are **true** or **false**.

| Statement | True | False |
|---|---|---|
| Hugh Town is a big city with a large population. | | |
| The Isles of Scilly are connected by bridges. | | |
| There are many different types of birds on the islands. | | |
| Shops, restaurants, bars and cafés rely on tourism to make money. | | |

1 mark

**30** *The Isles of Scilly have a **unique** climate . . .*

Which word is closest in meaning to *unique*?

Tick **one**.

strange ☐

special ☐

warm ☐

humid ☐

1 mark

**Questions 31–45 are about *Street Child* (see pages 81–83 in the reading booklet).**

**31** *. . . the long, high building with its rows of barred windows.*

What does the word *barred* suggest about the windows?

_____

_____
1 mark

**32** Why does Joseph say, *'It's the whole world, this place is.'*?

_____

_____
1 mark

**33** In which season is the extract set? Give **two** pieces of evidence from the text to support your answer.

_____

_____
2 marks

**34** Look at the paragraph *It was impossible to tell one day from the next . . .*

How does Jim know that he's been in the workhouse for a year?

_____

_____
1 mark

**35** *It was then that the little secret promise that had nestled inside him began to flutter into life like a wild thing.*

What is '*the little secret promise*' inside Jim?

_____
1 mark

**36** *The teacher **hauled** him off his stool . . .*

Which word below is closest in meaning to *hauled*?

Tick **one**.

poked ☐

pushed ☐

persuaded ☐

pulled ☐

1 mark

**37** Why does Jim say he doesn't mind when Mr Barrack is beating him?

_____

_____
1 mark

**38** Why do you think Mr Barrack winds a handkerchief around Jim's head and ties it under his chin?

_____

_____

1 mark

**39** When Mr Barrack had finished beating Jim, *he flung him like a bundle of rags across the desk.*

What **two** things does this suggest about Jim?

**1.** _____

_____

**2.** _____

_____

2 marks

**40** What reasons does Tip give for not going with Jim?

_____

_____

1 mark

**41** What do you think Jim is thinking when he reads the words *God is good. God is holy. God is just. God is love.* in the schoolroom?

_____

_____

1 mark

**42** Describe the relationship between the two main characters, Jim and Tip, throughout the extract.

Give examples from the text to support your answer.

_____

_____

_____

_____

2 marks

**43** Draw a line to match each event below to show the correct order from 1–6, as it appears in the extract.

| Mr Sissons asked for big boys to help. | | 1 |
| Jim asked Tip to run away with him. | | 2 |
| Jim tried to remember what life outside the workhouse was like. | | 3 |
| Tip shared his supper with Jim. | | 4 |
| Mr Barrack gave Jim a beating. | | 5 |
| Jim decided to climb over the wall and escape. | | 6 |

1 mark

**44** **Find** and **copy one** word which suggests Mr Barrack was pleased he had caught Jim talking.

*Mr Barrack sprang down from his chair, his eyes alight with anger and joy. 'You spoke!' he said to Jim, triumphant. 'It was you.'*

_____

1 mark

**45** When describing Jim's feelings throughout the extract, the writer has deliberately chosen language that will have an effect on the reader.

Explain the effect of the words used in the sentence below.

*Jim's wild thoughts drummed inside him, so loud that he imagined everyone would hear them.*

_____

_____

_____

1 mark

SET A

English grammar, punctuation and spelling

PAPER 1

# Key Stage 2

## English grammar, punctuation and spelling

**Paper 1:** questions

**Time:**

You have **45 minutes** to complete this test paper.

| Maximum mark | Actual mark |
|---|---|
| 50 | |

| First name | |
|---|---|
| Last name | |
| Date of birth | Day     Month     Year |

**1** What is the **word class** of the underlined words in the sentence below?

An elephant charged through the jungle, trampling the trees.

Tick **one**.

adjectives ☐

determiners ☐

nouns ☐

adverbs ☐

1 mark

**2** Tick the word that is closest in meaning to find out.

Tick **one**.

choose ☐

discover ☐

invite ☐

repeat ☐

1 mark

**3** Circle one verb in each underlined pair to complete the sentences using **Standard English**.

We **was / were** going to play outside on our bikes.

I **done / did** well in my maths test this morning.

1 mark

**4** Which sentence is punctuated correctly?

Tick **one**.

"wait for me!" shouted Orla. ☐

"Wait for me!" shouted Orla. ☐

"Wait for me"! shouted Orla. ☐

"Wait for me," shouted Orla! ☐

1 mark

**5** Which **verb form** completes the sentence?

Olivia and Sandip _____ sandcastles at the beach.

Tick **one**.

was building ☐

is building ☐

were building ☐

builded ☐

1 mark

**6** Which sentence below is a **command**?

Tick **one**.

We are baking a cake with Mum. ☐

You like chocolate cake, don't you? ☐

Put the flour and butter in the bowl. ☐

How hungry I am! ☐

1 mark

**7** Add the missing **full stops** and **capital letters** to the sentence below. The first one has been done for you.

N
~~n~~ottingham is located in the east midlands the river that runs through nottingham is called the river trent

1 mark

**8** Circle the **conjunction** in the sentence below.

Since it was very cold outside, Sam decided to fasten his coat.

1 mark

**9** Draw a line to match each **prefix** to the root word to make a new word.

| dis | haul |
| mis | honest |
| over | understood |

1 mark

**10** Insert **two apostrophes** in the correct places in the sentence below.

Emmas cat has had five kittens which are black, though one has white patches around its eyes; their neighbours dog will now have six cats to chase!

1 mark

**11** Use the **co-ordinating conjunctions** in the box to correctly complete the sentence below.
Use each conjunction **once**.

| or    but    and |

The books _____ DVDs need returning to the library on Monday _____ Tuesday, _____ remember it is closed each day for lunch.

1 mark

**12** Insert **two dashes** in the correct places in the sentence below.

William Shakespeare a famous author wrote the play 'Macbeth'.

1 mark

**13** Underline the **main clause** in the sentence below.

Although she is younger, my sister is much taller than me.

1 mark

**14** The incomplete sentences below are instructions in a recipe.
Add **two adverbials of time** to make the two sentences correct.
Remember to use correct punctuation.

_____ check you have the correct ingredients.

_____ turn the oven on to 180 degrees.

1 mark

**15** Choose **one** of the **question tags** below to complete the sentence.

| haven't you | haven't we | didn't you |

You've been learning about materials in science, _____? 1 mark

**16** Tick one box in each row to show if the sentence is in the **present progressive** or the **past progressive**.

| Sentence | Present progressive | Past progressive |
|---|---|---|
| While the band was playing, Jamie and I were dancing. | | |
| We are reading about the Romans in history. | | |
| The bell is ringing so we must go inside. | | |

1 mark

**17** Circle the **conjunction** in each sentence below.

The teacher was pleased with the children's work, so he gave them extra playtime.

Although it was summer, we felt it was really quite cold.

We visited some ancient caves when we were on holiday in France.

1 mark

**18** Insert a **comma** in the correct place in the sentence below.

Feeling confident the pianist played to a room full of people.

1 mark

**19** Circle the **adjective** in the sentence below.

Mum carefully topped the pudding with some whipped cream.

1 mark

**20** In the sentence below, what **word class** is the word they?

I wish they would be quiet now!

Tick **one**.

adjective ☐

preposition ☐

verb ☐

pronoun ☐

1 mark

**21** Which of the events below is the **most likely** to happen?

Tick **one**.

I will wash the car today. ☐

I should go to work. ☐

I might watch a film. ☐

I could play in the garden. ☐

1 mark

**22** Draw a line to match the words to the correct sentence type.

| How blue your eyes are | question |
| How old are you | statement |
| The music was very loud | command |
| Follow me outside, please | exclamation |

1 mark

**23** Circle the **pronoun** in the sentence below.

Zane ate his dinner and then he went outside to play.

1 mark

**24** Underline the **adverbial phrase** in the sentence below.

Later that evening, we said goodbye and began our journey home.

1 mark

**25** Add **three commas** in the correct places in the sentence below.

Mangoes kiwis apples pineapples and strawberries are all types of fruit.

1 mark

**26** Complete the sentence below with the **simple past tense** of the verbs in the boxes.

When the bell _____ , the teacher _____ into
                    ↑                                    ↑
                 to ring                              to come

the room and _____ us to be quiet.
                    ↑
                 to tell

1 mark

**27** Circle the two words that are **synonyms** in the passage below.

As dawn broke, Jake and Ushma strolled along the beach.

Sunrise was always their favourite time of the day on holiday.

1 mark

**28** Use the words below to complete the table.

| ancient | new | small | large | wealthy | poor |

|  | **Synonym** | **Antonym** |
|---|---|---|
| sad | unhappy | happy |
| rich |  |  |
| big |  |  |
| old |  |  |

1 mark

**29** Insert a pair of **brackets** in the sentence below.

The skateboard park located behind the playground is to be used by children who are over eight.

1 mark

**30** Circle the **adverb** in the sentence below.

Tim had worked hard on his spellings so he was disappointed he didn't finish the test.

1 mark

**31** Rewrite the sentence below in the **active** voice.

The ancient ruins were visited by the historians.

_____

1 mark

**32** Complete the sentence below with a **noun** formed from the verb calculate.

Jana used a _____ to work out the answer.

1 mark

**33** Circle the **preposition** in the sentence below.

The girl walked up the stairs.

1 mark

**34** Circle the **possessive pronoun** in the sentence below.

I had remembered my homework but Jamal had forgotten his.

1 mark

**35** Write out the words from the boxes below to make **one** sentence.
You can use the boxes in any order.
Remember to punctuate your answer correctly.

| came to visit us | at Christmas |
| who lives in France | My uncle |

_____

_____

1 mark

**36** Underline the **relative clause** in the sentence below.

The old lady who was shouting at her neighbour was feeling angry.

1 mark

**37** Write a suitable question to match the answer below.
Remember to use the correct punctuation.

**Question** _____

**Answer**   He takes the bus.

1 mark

**38** Which two sentences contain a **preposition**?

Tick **two**.

The spider crawled up the wall.  ☐

My mum doesn't really like spiders.  ☐

I put the spider in the garden.  ☐

Mum was so pleased she gave me a hug!  ☐

1 mark

**39** Write a **pronoun** in the space to make the sentence correct.

The boy ran across the playground but _____ was late again.

1 mark

**40** Complete the sentence below with a **contraction** that makes sense.

Why _____ you find your homework?

1 mark

**41** Rewrite the underlined verbs in the sentence below so that they are in the **past progressive** form.

While I danced on the stage, I could see that my parents clapped loudly.

[was dancing] [were clapping]

1 mark

**42** Add **inverted commas** to punctuate the speech below.

What time does the train leave the station? Mary asked the guard.

Three minutes past ten, the guard answered.

1 mark

**43** Which **punctuation mark** should be used in the place indicated by the arrow?

We ran and ran, even though we were out of breath, we simply couldn't miss that train.

Tick **one**.

- full stop ☐
- hyphen ☐
- semi-colon ☐
- comma ☐

1 mark

**44** Rewrite the sentence below so that it starts with a **subordinate clause**. Remember to punctuate your answer correctly.

I read a book while I was waiting to see the doctor.

_____

1 mark

**45** Which of the sentences uses **dashes** correctly?

Tick **one**.

The cat – fast asleep – on the rug – was keeping warm by the fire. ☐

The cat – fast asleep on the rug – was keeping warm by the fire. ☐

The cat fast asleep on the rug – was keeping warm – by the fire. ☐

The cat – fast asleep on the rug was keeping – warm by the fire. ☐

1 mark

**46** Write a **noun phrase** containing at least three words to complete the sentence below.
Remember to punctuate your answer correctly.

_____ asked me for directions to the library.

1 mark

**47** Which verb completes the sentence so that it uses the **subjunctive form**?

If I _____ to find a treasure chest, I'd share it with you.

Tick **one**.

did ☐

was ☐

were ☐

had ☐

1 mark

**48** Insert two **hyphens** in the correct places in the sentence below.

My mum, who is a well known author, has just written a new, action packed book.

1 mark

**49** Circle the **relative pronoun** in the sentence below.

When we reached the waterfall, which was our final destination, we made our camp and settled down for the night.

1 mark

**50** Use a **comma** and a **dash** in the correct places in the sentence below.

After we left the park we visited Ash and Paula the children who live opposite you.

1 mark

SET A

English grammar, punctuation and spelling

PAPER 2

# Key Stage 2

# English grammar, punctuation and spelling

## Paper 2: spelling

You will need to ask someone to read the instructions and sentences to you. These can be found on page 101.

**Time:**

You have approximately **15 minutes** to complete this test paper.

| Maximum mark | Actual mark |
|---|---|
| 20 | |

| First name | |
|---|---|
| Last name | |
| Date of birth | Day | | Month | | Year | |

# Spelling

**1** The actress performed _____ on stage.

**2** Our _____ little kitten had scratched the carpet.

**3** The flowers in the bathroom are _____.

**4** The doctor said the rash was highly _____.

**5** There is a _____ coming from the large window.

**6** The weather is very _____ today.

**7** The car in front was _____ right.

**8** James's dad is a very _____ sailor.

**9** Sam won a _____ he entered at school.

**10** I think I have done _____ homework now.

**11** Mangoes, pineapples, kiwis and oranges are all types of _____.

**12** Raj was _____ shocked to see his old friend again.

**13** The hotel sign said there was no _____.

**14** It is a year since Auntie Jan and Uncle Paddy were _____.

**15** The new _____ has introduced some interesting dishes.

**16** Grace passed the _____ carefully to Dan.

**17** I was very careful not to _____ my teacher's name.

**18** We _____ ran for help when we heard the alarm.

**19** Eventually, the _____ blew the final whistle.

**20** Our family eats _____ for breakfast.

# Key Stage 2

## English reading

Reading answer booklet

**SET B**

English reading

**Time:**

You have **one hour** to read the texts in the reading booklet (pages 85–92) and answer the questions in this answer booklet.

| Maximum mark | Actual mark |
|---|---|
| 50 | |

| First name | |
|---|---|
| Last name | |
| Date of birth | Day       Month       Year |

**Questions 1–12 are about *James and the Giant Peach*
(see pages 86–88 in the reading booklet).**

**1** How does the writer create a magical setting in the first paragraph?

_____

_____

1 mark

**2** Look at the paragraph beginning: *Almost without knowing what he was doing, as though drawn by some powerful magnet . . .*

What do the words *as though drawn by some powerful magnet* tell you?

_____

_____

1 mark

**3** *The tunnel was damp and **murky** . . .*

Which word is closest in meaning to *murky*?

Tick **one**.

| | |
|---|---|
| muddy | ☐ |
| gloomy | ☐ |
| soggy | ☐ |
| filthy | ☐ |

1 mark

**4** What evidence is there to suggest that James was not frightened as he crawled through the tunnel?

_____

_____

1 mark

**5** *The creatures, some sitting on chairs, others reclining on a sofa, were all watching him **intently**.*

Which word is closest in meaning to *intently*?

Tick **one**.

casually ☐

closely ☐

quickly ☐

strangely ☐

1 mark

**6** Draw a line to match each creature to the description James gives when he first meets them.

| Old-Green-Grasshopper | giant |
| Spider | enormous |
| Silkworm | as large as a large dog |
| Ladybird | thick and white |

1 mark

© 2018 Letts Educational, an imprint of HarperCollinsPublishers Ltd – not to be photocopied.

**7** *He glanced behind him, thinking he could bolt back into the tunnel . . .*

What does the word *bolt* tell you about how James is feeling?

_____

_____

2 marks

**8** Give **two** reasons why you think that the creatures might eat James.

1. _____

2. _____

2 marks

**9** Explain as fully as you can what the Ladybird means when she tells James, *'You are one of us now, didn't you know that?'*

_____

_____

1 mark

**10** Put a tick in the correct box to show whether each of the following statements is **true** or **false**.

|  | True | False |
|---|---|---|
| A fence surrounded the peach. |  |  |
| The tunnel was dry and cold. |  |  |
| James bumped his head on the stone in the middle of the peach. |  |  |
| James couldn't stand up because the peach wasn't big enough. |  |  |
| The creatures were at least the same size as James. |  |  |

1 mark

**11** What **effect** is the author trying to create in the sentence below?

*Four pairs of round black glassy eyes were all fixed upon James.*

_____

_____

_____

_____

2 marks

**12** Explain why this statement by the Centipede is funny.

*And meanwhile I wish you'd come over here and give me a hand with these boots. It takes me hours to get them all off by myself.*

_____

_____

_____  1 mark

**Questions 13–24 are about *About Floella* (see pages 89–90 in the reading booklet).**

**13** Why did Floella find growing up in South London challenging?

_____

_____
1 mark

**14** Look at the first paragraph.

**Find** and **copy one** word that is closest in meaning to 'move away'.

_____
1 mark

**15** Look at page 89.

How can you tell that Floella had a good relationship with her parents?

Give **three** pieces of evidence from the text.

1. _____

_____

2. _____

_____

3. _____

_____
3 marks

**16** What is the name of the first TV programme in which Floella starred?

_____

1 mark

**17** Find the year when each of the events below happened in Floella Benjamin's life. Write the answers in the grid below.

| Event | Date |
|---|---|
| Born | |
| Came to England | |
| Made her TV debut | |
| Started her own television production company | |
| Wrote *Coming to England* | |
| Trekked the Great Wall of China | |

2 marks

**18** In what order is the text written?

Tick **one**.

in order of importance ☐

in no particular order ☐

in chronological order ☐

1 mark

**19** In her book *Coming to England,* Floella talks about her feelings of rejection.

Why do you think Floella felt rejected?

_____

_____

1 mark

**20** Why is it a special achievement that Floella has run ten London Marathons?

_____

_____

1 mark

**21** Look at the last paragraph on page 90.

Which word tells us that Floella understands and shares the feelings of children?

_____
1 mark

**22** Summarise **three** ways that Floella has helped children's charities.

1. _____

_____

2. _____

_____

3. _____

_____
3 marks

**23** Put a tick in the correct box to show whether each of the following statements about Floella is **fact** or **opinion**.

|  | Fact | Opinion |
|---|---|---|
| She worked in a bank. |  |  |
| She loved her job on *Play School*. |  |  |
| She presented *Play School* for 12 years. |  |  |
| She has completed ten London Marathons. |  |  |
| She is a keen runner. |  |  |

1 mark

**24** Explain how Floella Benjamin's childhood influenced her to help young people across the world.

_____

_____

_____

2 marks

**Questions 25–35 are about *Macavity* (see pages 91–92 in the reading booklet).**

**25** *Macavity's a Mystery Cat: he's called the Hidden Paw —*

*For he's the master criminal who can **defy** the Law.*

Which word is closest in meaning to *defy*?

Tick **one**.

follow ☐

understand ☐

challenge ☐

attack ☐

1 mark

**26** Why is Macavity the bafflement of Scotland Yard and the despair of the Flying Squad?

_____

_____

1 mark

**27** The writer tells us that Macavity *breaks the law of gravity.*

What **two different** meanings are implied by this statement?

1. _____

_____

2. _____

_____

2 marks

**28** Look at the third verse.

This verse tells readers more information about Macavity's …

Tick **one**.

friends. ☐

personality. ☐

hobbies. ☐

appearance. ☐

1 mark

**29** Look at the third verse.

Which word tells you that Macavity is uncared for?

_____

1 mark

**30** Why do you think the poet repeats the words 'Macavity's not there'?

_____

_____

_____

1 mark

**31** *He always has an alibi, and one or two to spare:*

Explain what this line means.

_____

_____ 1 mark

**32** Who are Mungojerrie and Griddlebone?

_____

_____ 1 mark

**33** Put a tick in the correct box to show whether each of the following statements is **fact** or **opinion**.

|  | Fact | Opinion |
|---|---|---|
| It is fun watching Macavity cause trouble. |  |  |
| Macavity's a ginger cat. |  |  |
| His coat is dusty. |  |  |
| Macavity has no-one to care for him. |  |  |

2 marks

**34** What does the poem tell you about Macavity's character?

Describe **three** features of his character, using evidence from the text to support your answer.

_____

_____

_____

_____

_____

_____

3 marks

**35** Do you think the writer feels admiration or contempt for Macavity?

Use evidence from the text in your answer.

_____

_____

_____

_____

_____

_____

3 marks

SET B

English grammar, punctuation and spelling

PAPER 1

# Key Stage 2

## English grammar, punctuation and spelling

**Paper 1:** questions

**Time:**

You have **45 minutes** to complete this test paper.

| Maximum mark | Actual mark |
|---|---|
| 50 | |

| First name | |
|---|---|
| Last name | |
| Date of birth | Day | | Month | | Year | |

**1** Circle the **adjectives** in the sentence below.

The mysterious shadows darted quickly along the creepy path.

1 mark

**2** Which word completes the sentence below?

You cannot go on the field today _____ it is too muddy.

Tick **one**.

| | |
|---|---|
| however | ☐ |
| although | ☐ |
| because | ☐ |
| and | ☐ |

1 mark

**3** Insert an **apostrophe** in the correct place in each sentence to indicate possession.

The dogs tail was wagging.

Six boys coats were on the floor.

1 mark

**4** Rewrite the sentence below so that it begins with the **adverbial**. Use only the same words and remember to punctuate your answer correctly.

Kenzie blew out the candles after the singing.

_____

_____

1 mark

**5** Which sentence uses **capital letters** correctly?

Tick **one**.

On saturday, I went to a museum in London with Ushma. ☐

On Saturday, I went to a Museum in London with Ushma. ☐

On Saturday, I went to a museum in London with Ushma. ☐

On Saturday, i went to a museum in London with Ushma. ☐

1 mark

**6** Insert a **colon** in the correct place in the sentence below.

Mum put the following in my packed lunch cheese sandwiches, an apple and a yoghurt.

1 mark

**7** Which sentence is punctuated correctly?

Tick **one**.

Grace found a bouncy ball; in the garden she was fairly sure it was Jamal's. ☐

Grace found a bouncy ball in the garden; she was fairly sure it was Jamal's. ☐

Grace found a bouncy ball in the garden she was fairly sure; it was Jamal's. ☐

Grace found a bouncy ball in the garden she was fairly; sure it was Jamal's. ☐

1 mark

**8** The **prefix** dis– can be added to the word approve to make the word disapprove.

What does the word disapprove mean?

Tick **one**.

to make a mistake ☐

to find something unacceptable ☐

to prove something is right ☐

to think something is great ☐

1 mark

**9** Write a suitable **modal verb** in the sentence below.

They really _____ take more care.

1 mark

**10** Complete the sentence below with a **noun** formed from the verb celebrate.

We all joined in the _____ of the team's victory.

1 mark

**11** Circle the **conjunction** in the sentence below.

The girls were tired but it was too early to go to bed.

1 mark

**12** Circle the **object** in the sentence below.

The postman has just delivered this letter for you.

1 mark

**13** Underline the **relative clause** in the sentence below.

The ice cream van that is in the car park is very popular today.

1 mark

**14** Which two sentences below contain a **preposition**?

Tick **two**.

The truck drove under the bridge. ☐

Max dropped his ice cream so Mum bought him another. ☐

My best friend's uncle is a famous musician. ☐

Mum and I strolled along the canal path. ☐

1 mark

**15** Write a sentence using the word <u>cover</u> as a **verb**.
Do not punctuate the word.
Remember to punctuate your answer correctly.

_____
1 mark

Write a sentence using the word <u>cover</u> as a **noun**.
Do not change the word.
Remember to punctuate your answer correctly.

_____
1 mark

**16** Complete the sentence using suitable **pronouns**.

Rosie's homework was too hard for _____ and

_____ felt sad that _____

couldn't do it.

1 mark

**17** Which of the events in the sentences below is the **most** likely to happen?

Tick **one**.

We might go to the cinema tonight. ☐

He will go to school tomorrow. ☐

They could go camping at the weekend. ☐

I ought to tidy my bedroom. ☐

1 mark

**18** Which sentence is an **exclamation**?

Tick **one**.

I can't wait for the summer holidays ☐

I really love reading adventure books ☐

What a brilliant book that was ☐

What sort of books do you like reading ☐

1 mark

**19** Insert **a pair of brackets** in the correct place in the sentence below.

Mrs Jones the Year 5 teacher played the piano in school today.

1 mark

**20** Which underlined group of words is a **subordinate clause**?

Tick **one**.

Last Wednesday, <u>I went to see my cousins</u>. ☐

<u>My friend Lauren is coming</u> to stay the night. ☐

The flowers <u>that Dad bought for Mum</u> are purple, white and blue. ☐

<u>Dad is going fishing</u> even if it rains. ☐

1 mark

**21** Insert a **comma** in the correct place in the sentence below.

Hanging upside down the bat made loud noises as the night sky grew darker.

1 mark

**22** Complete the table by inserting a suitable **antonym**.

| Word | Antonym |
|---|---|
| stiff | |
| angry | |

1 mark

**23** Circle the two **adverbs** in the sentence below.

The monkeys noisily ate their food as the children watched excitedly.

1 mark

**24** Which sentence is a **statement**?

Tick **one**.

Ben has a new puppy called Sid ☐

Do you have any pets ☐

How I'd love to have a puppy ☐

Be careful how you hold the puppy ☐

1 mark

**25** Which one **prefix** can be added to all three words below to make their antonyms?
Write the prefix in the box.

behave

place

understand

☐

1 mark

**26** Write **two conjunctions** to complete the sentence below.

I like drawing _____ painting

_____ my sister prefers writing.

1 mark

**27** Rewrite the sentence below so that it begins with the **adverbial**. Remember to punctuate your sentence correctly.

We went to the cinema after tea.

_____

1 mark

**28** Complete the sentence below with the **simple past tense** of the verbs in boxes.

Mrs Shepherd _____ her class that the visitor
                    ↑
                 [to tell]

who _____ in assembly last year _____ this morning's
       ↑                                    ↑
   [to speak]                              [to be]

special guest.

1 mark

**29** Label each of the clauses in the sentence below as either **main** (M) or **subordinate** (S).

As we were walking to school, we saw Angus who was with his parents.

☐ ☐ ☐

1 mark

**30** Add the pronouns **I** and **me** to the sentences below to make them correct.

Noah and _____ went for a walk in the woods.

Our parents told my sister and _____ to hurry up.

1 mark

**31** Rewrite the sentence below in the **active**.
Remember to punctuate your answer correctly.

The hedges were cut by some hard-working gardeners.

_____

1 mark

**32** Insert a **pair of commas** in the correct place in the sentence below.

My grandfather always kind and understanding told me that

he would help me with my tricky homework.

1 mark

**33** Which of the sentences below uses the **semi-colon** correctly?

Tick **one**.

Ella played the piano; Alex played the flute. ☐

Ella played; the piano Alex played; the flute. ☐

Ella played; the piano; Alex played the flute. ☐

Ella; played the piano Alex; played the flute. ☐

1 mark

**34** What is the **subject** of the sentence below?

Every summer, Moira goes with her brother to Scotland.

Tick **one**.

- summer ☐
- Moira ☐
- brother ☐
- Scotland ☐

1 mark

**35** Circle one verb in each underlined pair to complete the sentence using **Standard English**.

I **did / done** a detailed piece of writing.

They **has / have** been playing outside.

1 mark

**36** Underline the **relative clause** in the sentence below.

Brighton, which is a seaside town, is located on the south coast of England.

1 mark

**37** Add the words from the boxes below to this sentence starter to make **one** sentence.
Remember to punctuate your answer correctly.

| when she got a puppy for her birthday | was thrilled |
| who loves dogs | Hayley |

My best friend _____

_____

1 mark

**38** Which sentence is punctuated correctly?

Tick **one**.

Liam is determined – to win this year's tennis tournament he's practised day and night. ☐

Liam is determined to win this year's tennis tournament – he's practised day and night. ☐

Liam is determined to win this year's tennis tournament he's practised – day and night. ☐

Liam is determined to win – this year's tennis tournament he's practised day and night. ☐

1 mark

**39** Replace the underlined words in the sentences below with their **contracted forms**.

They should have realised we had taken the dog out when he was not on his mat.

1 mark

**40** Insert the correct punctuation into this sentence.
The first one has been done for you.

During his stay on the farm jon saw some ducks a herd of goats and a huge pink pig

1 mark

**41** Circle the **possessive pronoun** in the passage below.

I handed my form into the teacher. Fergus has lost his so he has been given another one.

1 mark

**42** Rewrite the sentence below using **Standard English**.

I've not got none.

_____

1 mark

**43** Add a **suffix** to each verb below to make a **noun**.

| Verb | Noun |
|---|---|
| agree | |
| assist | |

1 mark

**44** Which punctuation mark should be used in the place indicated by the arrow?

Dad is anxious to get to work early this morning ↑ he will hear whether he has been promoted or not!

Tick **one**.

comma ☐

hyphen ☐

semi-colon ☐

apostrophe ☐

1 mark

**45** Insert a **comma** and a **dash** in the correct places in the sentence below.

As soon as we reached the cottage Mum and Dad lit a fire it was cold even for spring.

1 mark

**46** Rewrite the underlined verbs in the sentences below so that they are in the **present progressive form**.

Mum teaches yoga at the village hall.

[ is teaching ]

She intends to teach me some exercises.

[ is intending ]

1 mark

**47** Complete each sentence below with a word formed from the **root word** kind.

Kai showed great _____ when he helped the boy cross the road.

Our neighbour _____ looked after our dog when we went away.

1 mark

**48** Insert an **apostrophe** to show possession in the sentence below.

Annies mum worked at the school library.

1 mark

**49** Which word completes the sentence so that it uses the **subjunctive mood**?

The Head Teacher said, "If there _____ to be a fire, students should exit through the rear doors."

Tick **one**.

was ☐

were ☐

had ☐

going ☐

1 mark

SET B

English grammar, punctuation and spelling

PAPER 2

# Key Stage 2

# English grammar, punctuation and spelling

## Paper 2: spelling

You will need to ask someone to read the instructions and sentences to you. These can be found on pages 101–102.

**Time:**

You have approximately **15 minutes** to complete this test paper.

| Maximum mark | Actual mark |
|---|---|
| 20 | |

| First name | |
|---|---|
| Last name | |
| Date of birth | Day | | Month | | Year | |

# Spelling

1 Bea greeted the new member _____ .

2 Gran likes _____ during the long, winter months.

3 My ambition is to play football for my _____.

4 The chocolate cake was _____.

5 The _____ of Majorca is close to Spain.

6 The weather promises to be quite _____ this weekend.

7 You _____ you wouldn't tell.

8 We do not mind what type of _____ we stay in on holiday.

9 _____ can be mashed, chipped, boiled or baked.

10 After a _____ search, we still couldn't find the keys.

**11** We spoke _____ to the hysterical girl.

**12** Coffee and fizzy drinks usually contain _____.

**13** A visiting _____ played his guitar in assembly.

**14** Our teacher is good at _____ with our parents.

**15** My _____ feels full after lunch.

**16** Everyone has _____ fingerprints.

**17** We are always _____ when we walk down the cliff steps.

**18** Ned's _____ was the fastest.

**19** The gymnasts _____ their weight across the bars.

**20** The whole family is in _____ for our pet.

# Contents

## English reading booklets

### Set A
A Mad Tea Party ................................................................... 76
The Isles of Scilly ................................................................. 78
Street Child .......................................................................... 81

### Set B
James and the Giant Peach .................................................. 86
About Floella ........................................................................ 89
Macavity ............................................................................... 91

**Answers and mark scheme** ................................................ 93
**Spelling test administration** ............................................... 101

# Reading booklet

**SET A**

English reading

**READING BOOKLET**

## Contents

**A Mad Tea Party**

pages 76–77

**The Isles of Scilly**

pages 78–80

**Street Child**

pages 81–83

© 2018 Letts Educational, an imprint of HarperCollinsPublishers Ltd – not to be photocopied.

# A Mad Tea Party

*Alice has just drunk a magic potion, which has made her very small. It enables her to enter Wonderland, where nothing is ever quite as it seems!*

*The scene begins in the garden. There is a table under a tree in front of a house. The March Hare and the Hatter are having tea at the table. A dormouse sits between them.*

**Narrator:** The March Hare and the Mad Hatter are having tea, all squashed at one end of a very large table.

**Alice:** Hello, mind if I join you all?

**Hare, Hatter, Dormouse:** No room! No room!

**Alice:** What are you talking about, there's plenty of room.

*Alice sits down.*

**Hare:** Have some wine.

**Alice:** *(looking around the table)* I don't see any wine.

**Hare:** There isn't any.

**Alice:** *(in an angry voice)* Then it wasn't very civil of you to offer it!

**Hare:** It wasn't very civil of you to sit down without being invited.

**Alice:** I didn't know it was your table; it's laid for many more than three.

**Hatter:** *(looking up and down at Alice)* Your hair wants cutting.

**Alice:** You should learn not to make personal remarks. It's very rude!

**Narrator:** The characters continue arguing until the Hatter opens his eyes very wide and begins talking in riddles.

**Hatter:** Why is a raven like a writing desk?

**Alice:** I believe I can guess that.

**Hare:** Do you mean you think you can find the answer for it?

**Alice:** Exactly so.

**Hare:** Then you should say what you mean.

**Alice:** I do. At least, I mean what I say – that's the same thing you know.

**Hatter:** Not the same thing a bit! Why, you might just as well say that I like what I get is the same as I get what I like.

**Dormouse:** (*talking in a sleepy way*) I breathe when I sleep is the same thing as I sleep when I breathe!

**Hatter:** It is the same thing with you!

**Narrator:** The conversation drops, and the party sits silently for a minute.

(*The Hatter takes his watch out of his pocket and looks at it uneasily; he shakes it and holds it to his ear. He then dips it in his cup of tea and looks at it again.*)

**Hatter:** What day of the month is it?

**Alice:** (*thinks for a time*) The fourth.

**Hatter:** (*looking angrily at the March Hare*) Two days wrong! I told you butter wouldn't suit the works!

**Hare:** (*meekly*) It was the *best* butter.

**Hatter:** Yes, but some crumbs must have got in as well. You shouldn't have put it in with the bread-knife.

**Alice:** What a funny watch! It tells the day of the month, and doesn't tell what o'clock it is!

# The Isles of Scilly

## Location

The Isles of Scilly are a group of islands located 45 km (28 miles) off the coast of the Cornish peninsula.

## The Islands

The Isles of Scilly are made up of five inhabited and approximately 140 other islands. The largest of the islands is called St Mary's, with Tresco, St Martin's, St Agnes and Bryher being the others.

The main settlement on St Mary's is Hugh Town. This is a very small town with only a few shops, banks, restaurants, hotels and pubs. The population of Hugh Town is just over 1000.

## Travel

Because the Isles of Scilly are so small, very few people own cars. Locals usually walk or ride bicycles. Public transport is a boat service between the islands.

To reach the Isles of Scilly from the mainland, visitors need to travel on either a small aeroplane (Skybus) or a passenger ferry (*The Scillonian*). These methods of transport are both an amazing experience for travellers to the islands and the table below lists the advantages and disadvantages of each.

|  | Skybus | The Scillonian |
|---|---|---|
| **Advantages** | Travel to and from three different mainland airports | Cafés serving hot and cold food on board |
|  | Bird's-eye views of the islands | Often see dolphins, sea birds and basking sharks |
|  | Quick | Seaside views |
|  | Small and personal | Cheap |
| **Disadvantages** | Limited luggage allowed | Often rough seas and passengers may suffer motion sickness |
|  | More expensive | Longer journey |
|  | Flights can be cancelled because of high winds |  |

## Weather

The Isles of Scilly have a unique climate, with the mildest and warmest temperatures in the United Kingdom. The average annual temperature is 11.8°C (53.2°F) in comparison to London, where it is 11.6°C (52.9°F).

The winters in Scilly are relatively warm and the islands very rarely get frosts or snow. They are however windy, due to the full force of the wind off the Atlantic Ocean.

## Plants and Animals

The warm, humid climate of the Isles of Scilly allows a variety of rare plants and flowers to grow, which are not seen in other parts of the United Kingdom.

Some people describe the Scilly Islands as 'a large, natural greenhouse'. Even in winter, there are hundreds of different plants in bloom.

| Month | Jan | Feb | Mar | Apr | May | Jun | Jul | Aug | Sept | Oct | Nov | Dec |
|---|---|---|---|---|---|---|---|---|---|---|---|---|
| Average temp. °C (°F) | 8.0 (46.4) | 7.9 (46.2) | 8.8 (47.8) | 9.8 (49.6) | 12.0 (53.5) | 14.5 (58.1) | 16.5 (61.7) | 16.9 (62.5) | 15.5 (59.8) | 12.7 (54.8) | 10.3 (50.6) | 8.7 (47.6) |

Because of the warm temperatures, many birds migrate to Scilly. Some birds stop off on their way across the Atlantic Ocean, while others stay on the islands. There are many different types of birds on the islands, ranging from common birds such as sparrows, thrushes and gulls, to more unusual birds like puffins, cuckoos and wheatears.

## Tourism

The Isles of Scilly rely on tourism. The majority of shops, restaurants, bars and cafés earn money from visitors during the summer season. People travel to Scilly for many reasons. Quite often there are visitors who come on walking holidays, bird-watching trips and to relax on one of the quiet beaches.

Holidaymakers can choose accommodation suitable for their stay. The main islands have a choice of hotels, bed and breakfasts, self-catering cottages and camping facilities.

## Activities

Many people choose to participate in water sports, including sailing, kayaking, boating and fishing.

The islands are famous for their clear waters, which also make snorkelling and diving popular activities.

'Gig racing' is the main sport on the Isles of Scilly. Gigs are traditional working boats, which six or seven people sit inside and row. Many islanders take part in gig practices and races throughout the season.

People watch the races and cheer on the gigs from passenger boats that follow the race or they sometimes watch the finish from the quay on St Mary's. The Isles of Scilly host an annual gig championship; thousands of rowers from as far away as Holland flock to the island to race at this event.

## Historic Sites

The Isles of Scilly have many historic landmarks waiting to be explored, including castles, churches, lighthouses and ruins. There are art galleries and exhibitions, museums and often concerts to attend.

Probably the most impressive feature of the Isles of Scilly is its natural beauty; the swirling golden beaches, sand dunes, rocky coastlines and scenic views are well worth a visit.

# Street Child

'Joseph,' Jim asked the bent man one day out in the yard. 'How long have you been here?'

'Been here?' Joseph swung his head round and peered up at Jim. 'Seems like I was born here. Don't know nothing else, son. And I don't know all of this place neither.' He leaned against Jim so he could swing his head up to look at the long, high building with its rows of barred windows. 'I've not been in the room where the women go, though long ago I must have been in the baby-room, I suppose, with my ma. I've been in the infirmary wards. But there's all kinds of little twisty corridors and attics and places I've never been in Jim, and I don't want to, neither. It's the whole world, this place is.' He spread out his hands. 'Whole world.'

'It ain't, Joseph,' Jim told him. 'There's no shops here, and no carriages. And no trees.' He closed his eyes, forcing himself to try and remember what it was like outside. 'And there's no river. There's a great big river outside here.'

'Is there now?' said Joseph. 'I should like to see that river. Though to tell you the truth, Jim, I don't know what a river is. Tell you something.' He put his arm over Jim's shoulder to draw his ear closer to his own mouth. 'I don't want to die in here. If someone will let me know what day I'm going to die, I'll be grateful. I'll climb over that wall first.' He dropped his head down again and stared at his boots, whistling softly. 'Yes. That's what I'll do.'

Tip spluttered and nudged Jim, but Jim was looking up at the high walls that surrounded the workhouse, and at the bleak sky above it.

'How long have I been here, Tip?' he asked.

'How should I know?' Tip hugged his arms round himself. 'Keep moving, Jim. It's cold.'

It was impossible to tell one day from the next. They were all the same. School, sack-making, bed. The only thing that changed was the sky. Jim had seen the grey of snow clouds turning into the soft rain clouds of spring. He'd felt summer scorching him in his heavy, itchy clothes. And now the sky was steely grey again. The pump had long beards of ice on its handle.

'I've been here a year,' Jim said. It was then that the little secret promise that had nestled inside him began to flutter into life like a wild thing.

'I've got to skip off,' he let the mad thought rise up in him.

'If I don't, I'll be like Joseph. One day I won't remember whether I was born here or not. I won't know anywhere but here.'

During lessons that day, the old schoolmaster's voice droned on in the dim schoolroom. The boys coughed and shuffled in their benches, hunching themselves against the cold. Jim's wild thoughts drummed inside him, so loud that he imagined everyone would hear them. He leaned over to Tip and whispered in his ear, 'Tip, I'm going to run away today. Come with me?' Tip sheered round, and put his hand to his mouth. Mr Barrack sprang down from his chair, his eyes alight with anger and joy.

'You spoke!' he said to Jim, triumphant. 'It was you.'

Tip closed his eyes and held out his hand, but Jim stood up. He didn't mind. He didn't mind anything any more. The teacher hauled him off his stool and swung his rope round. It hummed as it sliced through the air.

'I don't mind,' Jim tried to explain, but this made Mr Barrack angrier than ever. At last he had caught Jim out, and he was beating him now for every time he had tried and failed. He pulled a greasy handkerchief out of his pocket and wound it round Jim's head, tying it tight under his chin.

'Just in case you feels like hollering,' he said. All the other boys stared in front of them. The rope stung Jim again and again and the beating inside him was like a wild bird now, throbbing in his limbs and in his stomach, in his chest and in his head, so wild and loud that he felt it would lift him up and carry him away.

When the schoolmaster had finished with him he flung him like a bundle of rags across the desk. Jim lay in a shimmer of pain and thrumming wings. He wanted to sleep. The bell rang and the boys shuffled out. Jim felt Tip's hand on his shoulder. He flinched away.

'That's what they do to the boys who skip off, Jim,' Tip whispered. 'They thrash 'em like that every day until they are good.'

Jim felt the wild thing fluttering again. 'Only if they catch them.'

'They always catch 'em. Bobbies catch 'em and bring 'em in, and they get thrashed and thrashed.'

Jim struggled to sit up. The stinging rolled down his body. 'Won't you come with me?'

'I daresn't. Honest, I daresn't. Don't go, Jim.'

Jim looked up at the great archways of the schoolroom. He knew the words off by heart. *God is good. God is holy. God is just. God is love.*

'I've got to,' he said. 'And I'm going tonight, Tip.'

---

Jim knew that he would have to make his break before old Marion did her rounds for the night. He had no idea how he was going to do it. At suppertime he stuffed his cheese in his pocket, and Tip passed his own share along to him.

At the end of the meal, Mr Sissons stood up on his dais. All the shuffling and whispering stopped. He moved his body slowly round, which was his way of fixing his eyes on everyone, freezing them like statues.

'I'm looking for some big boys,' he said. 'To help with the carpet-beaters.' He waited in silence, but nobody moved.

'Just as I would expect. A rush to help, when there is sickness in the wards.' A cold sigh seemed to ripple through the room. Mr Sissons laughed into it in his dry, hissing way. 'It might be cholera, my dears. That's what I hear. I've two thousand mouths to feed here, and someone has to earn the money, cholera or not. Somebody has to buy the medicines. Somebody has to pay for the burials.' He moved his body round in its slow, watchful circle again. 'Plenty of big strong boys here, eating every crumb I give them and never a word of thanks.' He stepped down from his dais and walked along the rows, cuffing boys on the back of their heads as he passed them. 'I want you all up in the women's wards straight after supper, and you don't come down again till all the carpets are done.'

'What's carpets?' asked Jim.

'Dunno,' Tip whispered, 'they come from the rich houses, and the women here beat 'em, and then they send them home.'

'I'm going with them,' Jim said suddenly, standing up as soon as the older boys did.

'A daft boy, you are,' said Tip. 'He asked for big boys.'

'You coming or not?' Jim darted off after the big boys and Tip ran after him.

# Reading booklet

SET **B**

English reading

READING BOOKLET

## Contents

**James and the Giant Peach**

pages 86–88

**About Floella**

pages 89–90

**Macavity**

pages 91–92

© 2018 Letts Educational, an imprint of HarperCollinsPublishers Ltd – not to be photocopied.

# James and the Giant Peach

The garden lay soft and silver in the moonlight. The grass was wet with dew and a million dewdrops were sparkling and twinkling like diamonds around his feet. And now suddenly, the whole place, the whole garden seemed to be *alive* with magic.

Almost without knowing what he was doing, as though drawn by some powerful magnet, James Henry Trotter started walking slowly towards the giant peach. He climbed over the fence that surrounded it, and stood directly beneath it, staring up at its great bulging sides. He put out a hand and touched it gently with the tip of one finger. It felt soft and warm and slightly furry, like the skin of a baby mouse. He moved a step closer and rubbed his cheek lightly against the soft skin. And then suddenly, while he was doing this, he happened to notice that right beside him and below him, close to the ground, there was a hole in the side of the peach.

It was quite a large hole, the sort of thing an animal about the size of a fox might have made.

James knelt down in front of it and poked his head and shoulders inside.

He crawled in.

He kept on crawling.

This isn't just a hole, he thought excitedly. It's a tunnel!

The tunnel was damp and murky, and all around him there was the curious bittersweet smell of fresh peach. The floor was soggy under his knees, the walls were wet and sticky, and peach juice was dripping from the ceiling. James opened his mouth and caught some of it on his tongue. It tasted delicious.

He was crawling uphill now, as though the tunnel were leading straight towards the very centre of the gigantic fruit. Every few seconds he paused and took a bite out of the wall. The peach flesh was sweet and juicy, and marvellously refreshing.

He crawled on for several more yards, and then suddenly – bang – the top of his head bumped into something extremely hard blocking his way. He glanced up. In front of him there was a solid wall that seemed at first as though it were made of wood. He touched it with his fingers. It certainly felt like wood, except that it was very jagged and full of deep grooves.

'Good heavens!' he said. 'I know what this is! I've come to the stone in the middle of the peach!'

Then he noticed that there was a small door cut into the face of the peach stone. He gave a push. It swung open. He crawled through it, and before he had time to glance up and see where he was, he heard a voice saying, 'Look who's here!' And another one said, 'We've been waiting for you!'

James stopped and stared at the speakers, his face white with horror.

He started to stand up, but his knees were shaking so much he had to sit down again on the floor. He glanced behind him, thinking he could bolt back into the tunnel the way he had come, but the doorway had disappeared. There was now only a solid brown wall behind him.

---

James's large frightened eyes travelled slowly around the room.

The creatures, some sitting on chairs, others reclining on a sofa, were all watching him intently.

Creatures?

Or were they insects?

An insect is usually something rather small, is it not? A grasshopper, for example, is an insect.

So what would you call it if you saw a grasshopper as large as a dog? As large as a *large* dog. You could hardly call *that* an insect, could you?

There was an Old-Green-Grasshopper as large as a large dog sitting on a stool directly across the room from James now.

And next to the Old-Green-Grasshopper, there was an enormous Spider.

And next to the Spider, there was a giant Ladybird with nine black spots on her scarlet shell.

Each of these three was squatting upon a magnificent chair.

On a sofa near by, reclining comfortably in curled-up positions, there was a Centipede and an Earthworm.

On the floor over in the far corner, there was something thick and white that looked as though it might be a Silkworm. But it was sleeping soundly and nobody was paying any attention to it.

Every one of these 'creatures' was at least as big as James himself, and in the strange greenish light that shone down from somewhere in the ceiling, they were absolutely terrifying to behold.

'I'm hungry!' the Spider announced suddenly, staring hard at James.

'*I'm* famished!' the Old-Green-Grasshopper said.

'So am *I*!' the Ladybird cried.

The Centipede sat up a little straighter on the sofa. '*Everyone's* famished!' he said. 'We need food!'

Four pairs of round black glassy eyes were all fixed upon James.

The Centipede made a wriggling movement with his body as though he were about to glide off the sofa – but he didn't.

There was a long pause – and a long silence.

The Spider (who happened to be a female spider) opened her mouth and ran a long black tongue delicately over her lips. 'Aren't you hungry?' she asked suddenly, leaning forward and addressing herself to James.

Poor James was backed up against the far wall, shivering with fright and much too terrified to answer.

'What's the matter with you?' the Old-Green-Grasshopper asked. 'You look positively ill!'

'He looks as though he's going to faint any second,' the Centipede said.

'Oh, my goodness, the poor thing!' the Ladybird cried. 'I do believe he thinks it's *him* that we are wanting to eat!' There was a roar of laughter from all sides.

'Oh dear, oh dear!' they said. 'What an awful thought!'

'You mustn't be frightened,' the Ladybird said kindly. 'We wouldn't dream of hurting you. You are one of us now, didn't you know that? You are one of the crew. We're all in the same boat.'

'We've been waiting for you all day long,' the Old-Green-Grasshopper said. 'We thought you were never going to turn up. I'm glad you made it.'

'So cheer up, my boy, cheer up!' the Centipede said. 'And meanwhile I wish you'd come over here and give me a hand with these boots. It takes me *hours* to get them all off by myself.'

# About Floella

Floella Benjamin was born in the Caribbean on an island called Trinidad on 23rd September 1949. Her father decided to emigrate to England and she came to join him in 1960, when she was 11 years old. Floella's family started their life in Great Britain in Beckenham, South London. Initially she found it very different to her life in Trinidad and growing up in two cultures was challenging.

Floella's mother (Marmie) was a great inspiration to her. She gave her lots of love and encouraged her to do well at school.

Floella always dreamed of becoming a teacher, but instead ended up working in a bank and then later starred in stage musicals. While Floella enjoyed being on stage, she also wanted to try working in television so she auditioned for a variety of roles. Her TV debut was in 1974 in a drama called *Within these Walls* and her success in the show landed her many more roles in TV dramas.

Floella then took on a new role as a presenter of *Play School*, a 1970s children's show. She loved this job and presented the programme for 12 years.

As well as acting and presenting, Floella also loves to sing. She began singing with her dad who had a jazz band.

She often sang with her dad's band and also with large classical orchestras.

In 1987 Floella started her own television production company.

Next page ▶▶▶

http://www.collins.co.uk/floellabenjamin

Floella has also starred in several pantomimes, worked on numerous radio programmes, narrated audio books and has done voiceovers for a range of adverts and commercials.

Since 1983, Floella has written over 25 children's books.

One book Floella is particularly proud of is one that has been made into a film. *Coming to England* was written in 1995 and is based on her own life. In the book Floella talks about what it's like to be different, to move countries and change cultures and her feelings of rejection. The drama *Coming to England* won a Royal Television Society Award in 2004.

Floella is a keen runner who has completed ten London Marathons for the children's charity Barnardo's. This achievement is even more special as until she turned 50 years old, Floella had never even run at all!

Trekking the Great Wall of China in 2004 in aid of NCH Action for Children is another one of Floella's achievements. She started this in the Gobi Desert and finished 400 km later where the Great Wall meets the Yellow Sea.

Today Floella's passion is for inspiring and helping children and young people. She is a patron and supporter of many charities, including Action for Children and the Sickle Cell Society. In 2008, Floella was inducted into the National Society for the Prevention of Cruelty to Children (NSPCC) Hall of Fame.

Floella supports and empathises with children and young people across the world. Through her charity work, her writing and personal attitudes, she strives to help young people find their identity and to understand where they come from. She hopes all children have a sense of belonging and learn to become proud of themselves.

# Macavity

Macavity's a Mystery Cat: he's called the Hidden Paw –
    For he's the master criminal who can defy the Law.
He's the bafflement of Scotland Yard, the Flying Squad's despair:
    For when they reach the scene of crime – *Macavity's not there!*

Macavity, Macavity, there's no one like Macavity,
    He's broken every human law, he breaks the law of gravity.
His powers of levitation would make a fakir stare,
    And when you reach the scene of crime – *Macavity's not there!*
You may seek him in the basement, you may look up in the air –
    But I tell you once and once again, *Macavity's not there!*

Macavity's a ginger cat, he's very tall and thin;
    You would know him if you saw him, for his eyes are sunken in.
His brow is deeply lined with thought, his head is highly domed;
    His coat is dusty from neglect, his whiskers are uncombed.
He sways his head from side to side, with movements like a snake;
    And when you think he's half asleep, he's always wide awake.

Macavity, Macavity, there's no one like Macavity,
    For he's a fiend in feline shape, a monster of depravity.
You may meet him in a by-street, you may see him in the square –
    But when a crime's discovered, then *Macavity's not there!*

He's outwardly respectable. (They say he cheats at cards.)
    And his footprints are not found in any file of Scotland Yard's.
And when the larder's looted, or the jewel-case is rifled,
    Or when the milk is missing, or another Peke's been stifled,
Or the greenhouse glass is broken, and the trellis past repair –
    Ay, there's the wonder of the thing! *Macavity's not there!*

And when the Foreign Office find a Treaty's gone astray,
    Or the Admiralty lose some plans and drawings by the way,
There may be a scrap of paper in the hall or on the stair –
    But it's useless to investigate – *Macavity's not there!*
And when the loss has been disclosed, the Secret Service say:
    'It *must* have been Macavity!' – but he's a mile away.
You'll be sure to find him resting, or a-licking of his thumbs,
    Or engaged in doing complicated long division sums.

Macavity, Macavity, there's no one like Macavity,
    There never was a Cat of such deceitfulness and suavity.
He always has an alibi, and one or two to spare:
    At whatever time the deed took place – MACAVITY WASN'T THERE!
And they say that all the Cats whose wicked deeds are widely known,
    (I might mention Mungojerrie, I might mention Griddlebone)
Are nothing more than agents for the Cat who all the time
    Just controls their operations: the Napoleon of Crime!

# Answers and mark scheme

## Set A English reading

### *A Mad Tea Party*

1. Accept either in the garden or in Wonderland. **(1 mark)**
2. She has just drunk a magic potion that makes her small. **(1 mark)**
3. …there's plenty of room. **(1 mark)**
4. the Hare **(1 mark)**
5. Because the Hare offers her some wine when there actually isn't any. **(1 mark)**
6. polite **(1 mark)**
7. ' …all squashed at one end of a very large table.' **(1 mark)**
8. Any one of the following points:
   - Alice thinks personal remarks are rude.
   - The Hatter's remarks are said very abruptly and to the point.
   - The Hatter's remarks are unprovoked.
   
   **(1 mark)**
9. The Mad Hatter begins talking in riddles. **(1 mark)**
10. Any one from: lessens; they become quiet; ends. **(1 mark)**
11. frustrated **(1 mark)**
12. He dips his watch in his cup of tea. **(1 mark)**
13. Any one from: it is a tea party which is very unusual; the characters are acting in strange ways; they are saying mad things; they are sitting squashed up; they are talking in riddles; they are offering wine which isn't there. **(1 mark)**
14. puzzle **(1 mark)**
15. Any one from: the Narrator sets the scene; moves the story forward; explains what's happening; introduces characters. **(1 mark)**
16. works **(1 mark)**
17. Because the best butter wouldn't be good for your watch. **(1 mark)**

### *The Isles of Scilly*

18. St Mary's **(1 mark)**
19. people live there **(1 mark)**
20. a small aeroplane (Skybus); a passenger ferry (*The Scillonian*)
    
    **(1 mark for both correct)**
21. A day visitor with no luggage would be best taking the aeroplane (Skybus) because it's quicker and they would have longer to spend in the Isles of Scilly. They have no luggage so can travel by aeroplane. They will get a good view of all the islands even though they will not get time to see them all on foot. They will be able to choose one of three airports to travel from on the mainland.
    
    **(1 mark for any point from above)**
    
    A family staying for a week who want to see dolphins swimming would be best taking the passenger ferry because they may be able to see dolphins (and basking sharks and sea birds) from the ferry. They are staying a whole week so have plenty of time to spend travelling to Scilly by boat. The family might want to buy food or drinks on board and, as the boat is cheaper, it will cost them less.
    
    **(1 mark for any point from above)**
22. Its warm, humid climate means that rare plants and flowers can grow, even in winter. **(1 mark)**
23. If there are high winds. **(1 mark)**
24. Participating: a participant would sit inside the gig; row; take part in races.
    Watching: a spectator would watch the race from a boat, or from the quay on St Mary's; cheer on the gigs.
    
    **(2 marks: 1 mark for one participating point, 1 mark for one watching point)**
25. Any three from: walking; bird watching; relaxing on beaches; water sports; visiting historic sites and art galleries; enjoying the wildlife / plants.
    
    **(1 mark for three correct answers)**
26. Any two from: walk; ride bicycles; by boat. **(1 mark)**
27. a travel leaflet **(1 mark)**
28. This phrase gives readers an image of the buildings waiting for people to visit them – really the buildings are just standing there – the author adds interest.
    
    **(1 mark)**

© 2018 Letts Educational, an imprint of HarperCollinsPublishers Ltd – not to be photocopied.

29.

| Statement | True | False |
|---|---|---|
| Hugh Town is a big city with a large population. | | ✓ |
| The Isles of Scilly are connected by bridges. | | ✓ |
| There are many different types of birds on the islands. | ✓ | |
| Shops, restaurants, bars and cafés rely on tourism to make money. | ✓ | |

**(1 mark for all correct)**

30. special **(1 mark)**

### Street Child

31. They are like prison windows. **(1 mark)**
32. He doesn't know life anywhere else. **(1 mark)**
33. Winter. Tip says it is cold; the pump had (long beards of) ice on its handle. **(2 marks)**
34. Any one from: He could tell the time of year by the weather; the sky changing; the light, and dark mornings and nights; he is aware of the change in the seasons. **(1 mark)**
35. His promise to himself to escape / run away. **(1 mark)**
36. pulled **(1 mark)**
37. Any one from: he knew he had plans to run away; he wasn't going to be there much longer, he had more important things to think about; this would be his last beating so he felt positive and thought he could deal with anything. **(1 mark)**
38. To stop him screaming / hollering (while he was being beaten / thrashed). **(1 mark)**
39. That he is as worthless as a bundle of rags; that he is as light as a bundle of rags. **(2 marks)**
40. He was afraid they'll get caught and get thrashed. **(1 mark)**
41. Any one from: there is no good, justice or love here; God is not looking after me **(1 mark)**
42. Any two from: Look out for each other: 'Don't go, Jim.' Care for each other: 'Tip passed his own share along to him.' Trust each other: Jim told Tip his plans – 'Tip, I'm going to run away today. Come with me?' Strong friendship: they suffer the workhouse together.
**(2 marks: award 1 mark for each correct point)**

43.

| | |
|---|---|
| Mr Sissons asked for big boys to help. | 1 |
| Jim asked Tip to run away with him. | 2 |
| Jim tried to remember what life outside the workhouse was like. | 3 |
| Tip shared his supper with Jim. | 4 |
| Mr Barrack gave Jim a beating. | 5 |
| Jim decided to climb over the wall and escape. | 6 |

**(1 mark for all correct)**

44. joy; triumphant
**(1 mark for either)**

45. Answers may vary. Example:
The words used make me think Jim's thoughts were crazy and like a drum banging loudly in his head. **(1 mark)**

## Set A English grammar, punctuation and spelling

**Paper 1: questions**

1. determiners **(1 mark)**
2. discover **(1 mark)**
3. We was / (were) going to play outside on our bikes.
   I done / (did) well in my maths test this morning. **(1 mark)**
4. "Wait for me!" shouted Orla. **(1 mark)**
5. were building **(1 mark)**
6. Put the flour and butter in the bowl. **(1 mark)**
7. ₦ottingham is located in the ₑast ₘidlands. ₜhe river that runs through ₙottingham is called the ᵣiver ₜrent. **(1 mark for all correct)**
8. (Since) it was very cold outside, Sam decided to fasten his coat. **(1 mark)**
9. dis — understood
   mis — haul
   over — honest
   **(1 mark)**
10. Emma's cat has had five kittens which are black, though one has white patches around its eyes; their neighbour's dog will now have six cats to chase! **(1 mark for both correct)**
11. The books **and** DVDs need returning to the library on Monday **or** Tuesday, **but** remember it is closed each day for lunch. **(1 mark for all correct)**
12. William Shakespeare – a famous author – wrote the play 'Macbeth'. **(1 mark)**
13. Although she is younger, <u>my sister is much taller than me.</u> **(1 mark)**
14. Any suitable adverbials of time, e.g. First / Firstly; Then; Next, followed by a comma. **(1 mark)**
15. You've been learning about materials in science, haven't you? **(1 mark)**

16. 

| Sentence | Present Progressive | Past progressive |
|---|---|---|
| While the band was playing, Jamie and I were dancing. | | ✓ |
| We are reading about the Romans in history. | ✓ | |
| The bell is ringing so we must go inside. | ✓ | |

**(1 mark for all correct)**

17. (so) Although (when) **(1 mark)**
18. Feeling confident, the pianist played to a room full of people. **(1 mark)**
19. whipped **(1 mark)**
20. pronoun **(1 mark)**
21. I will wash the car today. **(1 mark)**
22. How blue your eyes are — exclamation
    How old are you — question
    The music was very loud — statement
    Follow me outside, please — command
    **(1 mark for all correct)**
23. (he) **(1 mark)**
24. <u>Later that evening,</u> we said goodbye and began our journey home. **(1 mark)**
25. Mangoes, kiwis, apples, pineapples and strawberries are all types of fruit. **(1 mark for all correct)**
26. rang; came; told **(1 mark for all three correct)**
27. (dawn) (Sunrise) **(1 mark for both correct)**
28. 

| | Synonym | Antonym |
|---|---|---|
| sad | unhappy | happy |
| rich | wealthy | poor |
| big | large | small |
| old | ancient | new |

**(1 mark)**

29. The skateboard park (located behind the playground) is to be used by children who are over eight. (1 mark)
30. (hard) (1 mark)
31. The historians visited the ancient ruins. (1 mark)
32. calculator / calculation (1 mark)
33. (up) (1 mark)
34. (his) (1 mark)
35. My uncle, who lives in France, came to visit us at Christmas. **Or** My uncle who lives in France came to visit us at Christmas.
    (1 mark: accept dashes or brackets in place of commas)
36. The old lady who was shouting at her neighbour was feeling angry. (1 mark)
37. Any suitable question starting with a capital letter and ending with a question mark, e.g. How does Joel get to school? (1 mark)
38. The spider crawled up the wall. I put the spider in the garden.
    (1 mark for both correct)
39. he (1 mark)
40. Any one from: can't; won't; didn't; don't; couldn't; wouldn't (1 mark)
41. was dancing; were clapping
    (1 mark for both correct)
42. "What time does the train leave the station?" Mary asked the guard.
    "Three minutes past ten," the guard answered.
    (1 mark for both sentences correct)
43. semi-colon (1 mark)
44. While I was waiting to see the doctor, I read a book. (1 mark)
45. The cat – fast asleep on the rug – was keeping warm by the fire. (1 mark)
46. Answers will vary. Example: An old lady with white hair asked me for directions to the library. (1 mark)
47. were (1 mark)
48. My mum, who is a well-known author, has just written a new, action-packed book. (1 mark)
49. (which) (1 mark)
50. After we left the park, we visited Ash and Paula — the children who live opposite you. (1 mark)

**Paper 2: Spelling**
These are the correct spellings:
1. confidently
2. naughty
3. artificial
4. infectious
5. draught
6. changeable
7. indicating
8. competent
9. competition
10. enough
11. fruit
12. visibly
13. vacancy
14. married
15. chef
16. scissors
17. misspell
18. quickly
19. referee
20. cereal

## Set B English reading

### James and the Giant Peach
1. Accept answers that refer to: the atmosphere created by the moonlight; the 'soft and silver' garden; the dewdrops 'sparkling and twinkling like diamonds'. (1 mark)
2. That James seems to have no choice but to walk towards the peach. (1 mark)
3. gloomy (1 mark)
4. Any one from: He didn't act scared because he drank the peach juice as he crawled; He wouldn't have stopped every few seconds to take a bite out of the wall if he was frightened. (1 mark)
5. closely (1 mark)
6. Old-Green-Grasshopper — as large as a large dog
   Spider — enormous
   Silkworm — thick and white
   Ladybird — giant
   (1 mark)

7. Example: It tells you James is so scared that he wants to run as fast as he can towards the tunnel.

**(2 marks for answers that refer to James feeling frightened and wanting to escape quickly; 1 mark for reference to one of these points.)**

8. Answers may vary. Examples: The creatures / The Spider, the old-Green-Grasshopper, the Ladybird and the Centipede talk about how hungry they are; the Spider licked her lips; the creatures were all watching him intently. **(2 marks)**

9. Answers may vary. Examples: You have joined us now, you are just the same as us and we will treat you as our friend / family; You are no different from us – we are all here together; He has been enticed into the peach like they have. **(1 mark)**

10.

|  | True | False |
|---|---|---|
| A fence surrounded the peach. | ✓ |  |
| The tunnel was dry and cold. |  | ✓ |
| James bumped his head on the stone in the middle of the peach. | ✓ |  |
| James couldn't stand up because the peach wasn't big enough. |  | ✓ |
| The creatures were at least the same size as James. | ✓ |  |

**(1 mark for all five correct)**

11. The author is creating suspense. What is going to happen next? Telling us there were four creatures staring, the word 'fixed' creates the image – they were all looking at James, nothing else. The author is helping readers understand the anxiety James must be feeling.

**(2 marks: 1 mark for each point made)**

12. The Centipede has many feet so has a lot of boots to take off. **(1 mark)**

*About Floella*

13. Any one from: It was very different to her life in Trinidad; growing up in two cultures was challenging. **(1 mark)**
14. emigrate **(1 mark)**
15. Floella's mother (Marmie) was a great inspiration to her; her mother gave her lots of love (and encouraged her to do well at school); she often sang with her dad's jazz band.

**(3 marks: 1 mark for each)**

16. *Within these Walls* **(1 mark)**

17.

| Event | Date |
|---|---|
| Born | 1949 |
| Came to England | 1960 |
| Made her TV debut | 1974 |
| Started her own television production company | 1987 |
| Wrote *Coming to England* | 1995 |
| Trekked the Great Wall of China | 2004 |

**(2 marks: 1 mark if four or five answers are correct, 2 marks if all six answers are correct)**

18. in chronological order **(1 mark)**
19. Any one from: Because she was different / from a different country / from a different culture **(1 mark)**
20. Because she had never run at all until she turned 50. **(1 mark)**
21. empathises **(1 mark)**
22. Completed ten London Marathons for Barnardo's; trekked the Great Wall of China for NCH Action for Children; worked and raised money for the NSPCC.

**(3 marks: 1 mark for each point)**

23.

|  | Fact | Opinion |
|---|---|---|
| She worked in a bank. | ✓ |  |
| She loved her job on *Play School*. |  | ✓ |
| She presented *Play School* for 12 years. | ✓ |  |
| She has completed ten London Marathons. | ✓ |  |
| She is a keen runner. |  | ✓ |

**(1 mark for all correct)**

24. Because Floella moved to a new culture when she was a child, she is aware of the difficulties children face in this situation; she wants to help children in a similar position; to help them find their identity; and wants to help them to understand where they came from.

**(2 marks: 1 mark for any two points made)**

*Macavity*

25. challenge **(1 mark)**

26. Any one from: Because when they get to crime scene, Macavity is not there; they can't catch Macavity **(1 mark)**
27. The law of gravity is what makes us stay on the ground / stops us floating about in space but Macavity is never there so it is like even gravity can't keep him on the ground.
It is another law that Macavity breaks, as well as every human law.
**(2 marks: award 1 mark for each point)**
28. appearance **(1 mark)**
29. neglect **(1 mark)**
30. Any one from: Macavity's absence is the main point of the poem; Repetition of the words emphasises Macavity's absence. **(1 mark)**
31. There is always someone, or more than one person, who will cover for Macavity / say they were with Macavity, so he couldn't have committed the crime. **(1 mark)**
32. They are cats who work for Macavity / who are Macavity's agents. **(1 mark)**
33. 

|  | Fact | Opinion |
|---|---|---|
| It is fun watching Macavity cause trouble. |  | ✓ |
| Macavity's a ginger cat. | ✓ |  |
| His coat is dusty. | ✓ |  |
| Macavity has no-one to care for him. |  | ✓ |

**(2 marks for all correct; 1 mark for three correct)**

34. He commits crimes / is a thief / is a fiend / is a master criminal because the poet says he can defy the Law.
He is smart / clever because he is never caught by the police / Scotland Yard / the Flying Squad / the Foreign Office / the Admiralty / the Secret Service / can do long division sums.
He is a cheat / deceitful because he cheats at cards.
**(3 marks: award 1 mark for each point made with supporting evidence, up to a maximum of 3 marks)**

35. Answers will vary. Examples:
Admiration because the writer calls him a 'master criminal', which shows he thinks he is good at what he does. He is able to baffle Scotland Yard, who should be able to catch a mere cat.
**(3 marks)**
Admiration because the writer says there's no one like Macavity, as if to say there is no one as good as he is. He also says 'there's the wonder of the thing!' which sounds like the writer thinks Macavity's ability to disappear is wonderful.
**(3 marks)**
Admiration because the writer says that all the other criminal cats are 'nothing more than agents' for Macavity, which means that Macavity is the boss who 'controls their operations'.
**(2 marks)**
Contempt because the writer says 'he's broken every human law' and he's a 'fiend' and a 'monster'. **(2 marks)**
Contempt because the writer says he is a cat of 'such deceitfulness and suavity'. **(1 mark)**

## Set B English grammar, punctuation and spelling

**Paper 1: questions**
1. (mysterious) (creepy) **(1 mark for both correct)**
2. because **(1 mark)**
3. The dog's tail was wagging.
Six boys' coats were on the floor.
**(1 mark for both correct)**
4. After the singing, Kenzie blew out the candles. **(1 mark)**
5. On Saturday, I went to a museum in London with Ushma. **(1 mark)**
6. Mum put the following in my packed lunch: cheese sandwiches, an apple and a yoghurt. **(1 mark)**
7. Grace found a bouncy ball in the garden; she was fairly sure it was Jamal's. **(1 mark)**
8. to find something unacceptable **(1 mark)**
9. Any suitable modal verb, e.g. should; ought (to); could **(1 mark)**
10. celebration **(1 mark)**
11. (but) **(1 mark)**

12. (this letter) **(1 mark)**
13. The ice cream van <u>that is in the car park</u> is very popular today. **(1 mark)**
14. The truck drove under the bridge.
    Mum and I strolled along the canal path.
    **(1 mark for both correct)**
15. Answers will vary. Examples:
    Dad began to cover his meal with sauce.
    **(1 mark)**
    The cook placed a cover on the pan.
    **(1 mark)**
16. Rosie's homework was too hard for **her** and **she** felt sad that **she** couldn't do it.
    **(1 mark for all correct)**
17. He will go to school tomorrow. **(1 mark)**
18. What a brilliant book that was **(1 mark)**
19. Mrs Jones (the Year 5 teacher) played the piano in school today. **(1 mark)**
20. The flowers <u>that Dad bought for Mum</u> are purple, white and blue. **(1 mark)**
21. Hanging upside down, the bat made loud noises as the night sky grew darker. **(1 mark)**
22. Any suitable words, e.g.

| Word | Antonym |
| --- | --- |
| stiff | bendy |
| angry | calm |

**(1 mark for both correct)**

23. (noisily) (excitedly) **(1 mark for both correct)**
24. Ben has a new puppy called Sid **(1 mark)**
25. mis **(1 mark)**
26. I like drawing **and** painting **but / although** my sister prefers writing.
    **(1 mark for both correct)**
27. After tea, we went to the cinema.
    **(1 mark for correct adverbial and correct punctuation)**
28. told; spoke; was **(1 mark for all correct)**
29. 
    As we were walking to school , we saw Angus who was with his parents.
    [S]              [M]              [S]
    **(1 mark for all correct)**

30. Noah and **I** went for a walk in the woods.
    Our parents told my sister and **me** to hurry up. **(1 mark)**
31. Some hard-working gardeners cut the hedges.
    **(1 mark)**
32. My grandfather, always kind and understanding, told me that he would help me with my tricky homework.
    **(1 mark for both commas correctly placed)**
33. Ella played the piano; Alex played the flute. **(1 mark)**
34. Moira **(1 mark)**
35. (did) ; (have) **(1 mark for both correct)**
36. Brighton, <u>which is a seaside town</u>, is located on the south coast of England. **(1 mark)**
37. My best friend, Hayley, who loves dogs, was thrilled when she got a puppy for her birthday.
    **Or** My best friend Hayley, who loves dogs, was thrilled when she got a puppy for her birthday.
    **(1 mark)**
38. Liam is determined to win this year's tennis tournament – he's practised day and night.
    **(1 mark)**
39. should've; we'd; wasn't **(1 mark for all correct)**
40. During his stay on the farm, Jon saw some ducks, a herd of goats and a huge, pink pig.
    Accept a colon after 'saw'. **(1 mark)**
41. (his) **(1 mark)**
42. I have not got any / I've not got any / I haven't got any. **(1 mark)**
43. 

| Verb | Noun |
| --- | --- |
| agree | agreement |
| assist | assistant / assistance |

**(1 mark for both correct)**

44. semi-colon **(1 mark)**
45. As soon as we reached the cottage, Mum and Dad lit a fire – it was cold even for spring.
    **(1 mark)**
46. is teaching; is intending
    **(1 mark for both correct)**
47. kindness; kindly
    **(1 mark for both correct)**
48. Annie's mum worked at the school library.
    **(1 mark)**
49. were **(1 mark)**

© 2018 Letts Educational, an imprint of HarperCollinsPublishers Ltd – not to be photocopied.

99

**Paper 2: Spelling**

These are the correct spellings:
1. awkwardly
2. knitting
3. country
4. delicious
5. island
6. favourable
7. promised
8. accommodation
9. potatoes
10. thorough
11. calmly
12. caffeine
13. musician
14. communicating
15. stomach
16. unique
17. cautious
18. vehicle
19. transferred
20. mourning

# Spelling test administration

The instructions below are for the spelling tests.
Read the following instruction out to your child:
*I am going to read 20 sentences to you. Each sentence has a word missing. Listen carefully to the missing word and fill this in the answer space, making sure that you spell it correctly.*
*I will read the word, then the word within a sentence, then repeat the word a third time.*
You should now read the spellings three times, as given below. Leave at least a 12-second gap between spellings. At the end, read all the sentences again, giving your child the chance to make any changes they wish to their answers.

## Set A English grammar, punctuation and spelling

**Paper 2: spelling**

**Spelling 1**: The word is **confidently**.
The actress performed **confidently** on stage.
The word is **confidently**.

**Spelling 2**: The word is **naughty**.
Our **naughty** little kitten had scratched the carpet.
The word is **naughty**.

**Spelling 3**: The word is **artificial**.
The flowers in the bathroom are **artificial**.
The word is **artificial**.

**Spelling 4**: The word is **infectious**.
The doctor said the rash was highly **infectious**.
The word is **infectious**.

**Spelling 5**: The word is **draught**.
There is a **draught** coming from the large window.
The word is **draught**.

**Spelling 6**: The word is **changeable**.
The weather is very **changeable** today.
The word is **changeable**.

**Spelling 7**: The word is **indicating**.
The car in front was **indicating** right.
The word is **indicating**.

**Spelling 8**: The word is **competent**.
James's dad is a very **competent** sailor.
The word is **competent**.

**Spelling 9**: The word is **competition**.
Sam won a **competition** he entered at school.
The word is **competition**.

**Spelling 10**: The word is **enough**.
I think I have done **enough** homework now.
The word is **enough**.

**Spelling 11**: The word is **fruit**.
Mangoes, pineapples, kiwis and oranges are all types of **fruit**.
The word is **fruit**.

**Spelling 12**: The word is **visibly**.
Raj was **visibly** shocked to see his old friend again.
The word is **visibly**.

**Spelling 13**: The word is **vacancy**.
The hotel sign said there was no **vacancy**.
The word is **vacancy**.

**Spelling 14**: The word is **married**.
It is a year since Auntie Jan and Uncle Paddy were **married**.
The word is **married**.

**Spelling 15**: The word is **chef**.
The new **chef** has introduced some interesting dishes.
The word is **chef**.

**Spelling 16**: The word is **scissors**.
Grace passed the **scissors** carefully to Dan.
The word is **scissors**.

**Spelling 17**: The word is **misspell**.
I was very careful not to **misspell** my teacher's name.
The word is **misspell**.

**Spelling 18**: The word is **quickly**.
We **quickly** ran for help when we heard the alarm.
The word is **quickly**.

**Spelling 19**: The word is **referee**.
Eventually, the **referee** blew the final whistle.
The word is **referee**.

**Spelling 20**: The word is **cereal**.
Our family eats **cereal** for breakfast.
The word is **cereal**.

© 2018 Letts Educational, an imprint of HarperCollinsPublishers Ltd – not to be photocopied.

# Set B English grammar, punctuation and spelling

**Paper 2: spelling**

**Spelling 1**: The word is **awkwardly**.
Bea greeted the new member **awkwardly**.
The word is **awkwardly**.

**Spelling 2**: The word is **knitting**.
Gran likes **knitting** during the long, winter months.
The word is **knitting**.

**Spelling 3**: The word is **country**.
My ambition is to play football for my **country**.
The word is **country**.

**Spelling 4**: The word is **delicious**.
The chocolate cake was **delicious**.
The word is **delicious**.

**Spelling 5**: The word is **island**.
The **island** of Majorca is close to Spain.
The word is **island**.

**Spelling 6**: The word is **favourable**.
The weather promises to be quite **favourable** this weekend.
The word is **favourable**.

**Spelling 7**: The word is **promised**.
You **promised** you wouldn't tell.
The word is **promised**.

**Spelling 8**: The word is **accommodation**.
We do not mind what type of **accommodation** we stay in on holiday.
The word is **accommodation**.

**Spelling 9**: The word is **potatoes**.
**Potatoes** can be mashed, chipped, boiled or baked.
The word is **potatoes**.

**Spelling 10**: The word is **thorough**.
After a **thorough** search, we still couldn't find the keys.
The word is **thorough**.

**Spelling 11**: The word is **calmly**.
We spoke **calmly** to the hysterical girl.
The word is **calmly**.

**Spelling 12**: The word is **caffeine**.
Coffee and fizzy drinks usually contain **caffeine**.
The word is **caffeine**.

**Spelling 13**: The word is **musician**.
A visiting **musician** played his guitar in assembly.
The word is **musician**.

**Spelling 14**: The word is **communicating**.
Our teacher is good at **communicating** with our parents.
The word is **communicating**.

**Spelling 15**: The word is **stomach**.
My **stomach** feels full after lunch.
The word is **stomach**.

**Spelling 16**: The word is **unique**.
Everyone has **unique** fingerprints.
The word is **unique**.

**Spelling 17**: The word is **cautious**.
We are always **cautious** when we walk down the cliff steps.
The word is **cautious**.

**Spelling 18**: The word is **vehicle**.
Ned's **vehicle** was the fastest.
The word is **vehicle**.

**Spelling 19**: The word is **transferred**.
The gymnasts **transferred** their weight across the bars.
The word is **transferred**.

**Spelling 20**: The word is **mourning**.
The whole family is in **mourning** for our pet.
The word is **mourning**.